"Miss U"
Angel of the Underground

Margaret Utinksy

First published in 1948.

This edition published in 2017.

Table of Contents

Foreword

When, on December 8, 1941, a few hours after the attack on Pearl Harbor, the Japanese forces made an equally unprovoked, dastardly attack on the Philippines without declaration of war, those Islands were defended by less than twenty thousand American troops, by one cavalry, two infantry, and two coast artillery regiments of Philippine Scouts which helped to man the heavy armament of the fortified islands at the entrance to Manila Bay. The Philippine Army, only partially mobilized, partially equipped, partially trained and officered in the lower grades by partially trained Philippine Army officers, was initially not of much use in the defense of the Islands. Later, after some battle experience they did quite well.

It is to be remembered that at the time of the sneak attacks on Pearl Harbor and the Philippines, the Japanese had an Ambassador, Extraordinary and Plenipotentiary, in Washington who was supposed to be negotiating terms for the settlement of differences between our country and Japan, and at the very time, Japanese planes and fleets were approaching Hawaii and the Philippines. The Japs were running true to form.

After having destroyed the greater part of our Air Force in the Philippines on the first day (December 8), about 150,000 Japs, strongly supported by warships and airplanes, to be opposed by only 30,000 troops, all of the untrained Philippine Army except one regiment of Philippine Scout Cavalry, landed in North Luzon. Landings were also made in South Luzon with the proportion of attackers to defenders about the same as in the north. As well attempt to dam Niagara Falls with mud, as to stop the hostile horde with the means available. Withdrawn by order of the High Command to Bataan, Americans and Filipinos made a gallant stand on Bataan and Corregidor until starvation, lack of supplies and ammunition and overwhelming enemy forces finally spelt their doom.

As many as could do so took to the hills and became guerrillas. The remainder underwent the "Death March" out of Bataan and the horrors, starvation, and in some cases torture of prison camps for over two, and for those who were moved to Japan and Manchuria, for over three years. How the prisoners of war who remained on Luzon were helped by the intrepid souls who stayed outside of the barbed wire is amply set forth in these pages. Those who were discovered helping the prisoners suffered unspeakable tortures and in many cases death.

And the guerrillas rendered valuable services. They continually harassed the enemy, gained valuable information and were ready to and did assist our forces when they made the great counter attack from the south. If these guerrillas were captured, they were put to death after unspeakable torture, which happened to several officers well known to the undersigned. God rest their gallant souls.

"Miss U" took every chance, ran every risk, and underwent torture in order to help the poor men behind the barbed wire, and finally had to go to the hills and join the guerrillas. Her gallantry and intrepidity were worthy of the best traditions of our country.

— J. M. Wainwright General, U.S.A. (Retired)

"But I tell you, my lord fool, out of this nettle,
Danger, we pluck this flower, safety"
Shakespeare

Enemy Alien

It was January the second when the Japanese came into Manila. Through the nearly closed windows of my second-floor apartment I peered out at them. At every street corner Japanese officers with interpreters were setting up card tables, checking everyone who passed, searching for enemy aliens. Enemy alien! That was a queer thing for an American to be in the Philippines.

My radio was tuned low and over it came a stream of orders. All British and Americans were to remain at home until they could be investigated and registered. That meant going into internment camp. The internment was a formality and it would not last long. Just a matter of three or four days, they said.

I was born Peggy Doolin, and having Irish blood, I don't like being told what to do. Thank God, I have never followed advice, even when it was good. To obey instructions and go tamely into an internment camp seemed like the sensible thing to do, but for the life of me I could not see what use I would be to myself or to anyone else cooped up there. So I decided to remain hidden — barricaded, rather, in my apartment until it was safe to go out and discover for myself what was going on and how I could get to Bataan where my husband was. For from the moment the inconceivable thing happened and the Japanese arrived, there was just one thought in my mind — to find Jack.

At least, this would not last. Manila was an open city and the Japanese were only passing through. They said so. Everyone said so. By morning, perhaps, they would be gone as swiftly as they had come.

I had been working as a volunteer nurse with the Red Cross and running a servicemen's canteen in my spare time. All that day I had been at the hospital. At six in the evening we were ordered home. On my way I was stopped by the crowds gathering on the street and inquired idly of a man standing near me, "Do you think it is true that the Japs will come in tonight?"

He gave me a strange look and said in a kind of choked voice, "What the hell do you think that is?"

Right in front of me a motorcycle was parked. The driver got off and removed his goggles. Then I saw the Japanese flags. They were already in

Manila — they were beside me. I could not take it in. I kept telling myself, "Here they are; they have us," but it made no sense.

A mob of people sprang up from nowhere and began pushing their way into the Bay View Hotel. I was caught up and swept along into the lobby and the elevator. We had reached the seventh floor before I could fight my way off — and I walked straight back into yesterday.

It was the cocktail hour, and on the seventh floor of the hotel Americans were ordering highballs and getting up card games. They did not even know the Japanese were in Manila! By the time the excited, disheveled crowd had unloaded from the elevator, they had begun to get the idea.

Almost at once rumors began to spread. No one seemed to know what to do — I didn't either, for that matter, except that it would not be what I was told to do. I ran down all seven flights and was trying to get out of the lobby when an American stopped me.

"Where are you going?"

"Home," I said.

"You can't," he protested. "I hear the Japs are going to start shooting at eight o'clock."

"Well," I said impatiently, "I still have fifteen minutes," and I loped down the street.

My apartment was in the Ermita district of Manila, on a narrow street lined with palms and acacias. It had originally been a one-family apartment but when the war clouds began to gather and people began pouring into the city from outlying districts for safety, it had been converted into a two-family apartment. Perhaps I had better describe it, as its arrangement was unusual and so many things happened there.

A big iron fence ran in front of the building, with a separate gate for each apartment. I lived on the second floor and across the stairs there was a folding gate with a padlock. I had a living room that faced the street, a bedroom, bath, and a kitchenette which had been made from what originally was a dressing room.

The windows in Manila are made of shell instead of glass; when they are closed you cannot see in or out and at night the light from inside makes a pink glow, so that the houses look like shining Christmas cards. These shell windows slide to the side instead of moving up and down and inside there are Venetian blinds. Therefore, by leaving the windows open very slightly and keeping the Venetian blinds down I could watch what went on in the street but no one could see into the apartment. The tenant who

occupied the first floor had moved away and as long as t'
vacant, I hoped the Japanese would think mine was too.

All that night I stood at the windows and watched ...
pour into the city. And all the next day. On the second night the ...
soldiers were bedded down along the street. Canvases were stretched for them, canvases marked "U.S." and soaked with blood from the fighting south of Manila.

It is surprising what one can learn about a neighborhood while living in a house that is supposed to be empty. On that second day of the occupation I noticed a lot of unusual activity going on in a house across the street from my apartment. It had been occupied by an American woman who had fled from the place to the home of a friend when the invasion started and who later went to an internment camp. Her house had been left in the care of her Number One boy, a Filipino who seemed to be grief-stricken when she left, and kept saying that he knew the Japanese would kill him.

But this morning he did not look scared. He and his wife were standing at the gate, all dressed up in their Sunday best. Then a couple of high-ranking Japanese officers appeared, escorted by a Japanese who owned a lumberyard in Manila. The Japanese were bearing gifts wrapped in silk; there was much gold braid, there were handshakes and bows and hisses all over the place. Then they went inside for a big feast. The Filipino Number One boy was a collaborator in excellent standing with the enemy and there was not a thing I could do about it — then.

Down the street there lived a Spanish-Jewish mestiza, a woman of ill repute but well educated. When the Japanese came in, she promptly attached herself to them. From my second-floor lookout I saw her riding with them, and it was clear that she was giving them information. And early every morning an American newspaper woman came hurrying past my house — the only American who seemed free to come and go as she pleased after the first few days. I began to wonder about her.

The days crept by and I remained in hiding, with Japs all around me. By now, of course, I knew they had come to stay. And how grateful I was for having disobeyed orders and taken that apartment.

The *Washington*, the last ship to leave the Philippines carrying Army wives, had sailed from Manila, and I was supposed to be on it. Over my protest, my furniture was packed up and taken to the pier. I said I was not going.

won't be long," my husband tried to comfort me. "We'll make short ork of the Japs if they do come. You'll be back before you know it."

"Before *you* know it," I corrected him. "I won't be one of those thousands of women back in the States who have to sit and wonder every minute what is happening here in the Islands. What can I do over there? Here at least I could help if anything happened." That was the way we talked then — "*if* anything happened."

I knew I would not go. So did Jack. But because he was a law-abiding man, he turned tail and fled before the ship pulled out. I stood at the head of the gangplank until the very last minute, all dressed for traveling and plastered with orchids. The gong rang for "All ashore that's going ashore." The men got off and a few Spanish and Filipinos who had come to say goodbye to their friends. I calmly marched down the gangplank with them and went to the end of the pier.

The boat backed out, turned, went through breakwater. My heart ached for the men standing on the pier, taking a last look at their wives through field glasses. Beside me stood General Jonathan Wainwright, watching as the ship moved out of sight. That was my last glimpse of him until 1942, when I saw him being taken from the University club to a closed car and on his way to Tarlac, a prisoner of war.

My furniture and dishes stood on the pier and I arranged at once to have them sent back to me. Then I went to the hotel where my husband was waiting. He was a civil engineer, working for the Government, and he had to go back to Bataan.

"Be sure to stay on at the hotel," he told me. "You'll be safe here."

I did nothing of the sort. I found this apartment and fixed it up. In the hotel I would have been picked up at once and interned. What I had not figured on, of course, was that instead of hiding in the apartment for a day or two it was to be ten weeks before the night came when I dared to creep outside and learn what was happening in Manila.

At least I was in no danger of starving. Earlier in the month, the Army and Navy had thrown their commissaries open to the public, urging people to take whatever they could use. The rest would be destroyed to prevent its falling into Japanese hands. The departure of the Americans would be only temporary — how sure we all were of that! — and I wanted to be set to start a canteen again, so I thought it would be a sound idea to put in as many supplies as I could.

I chartered a fleet of eight taxicabs and got hold of some husky Filipino boys. Seven times I filled those cabs as full as they could be stacked. An American Negro woman, Mrs. Margaret Silverton, who owned a laundry, entered into the spirit of the thing and lent me her laundry truck. By the time I got through, my apartment was stacked to the ceiling with everything I could get my hands on: cases of Vienna sausage, corned beef, sardines, vegetables, juices; crackers, flour and sugar; and — most important of all — drugs.

For ten weeks I hid in that apartment, knowing only what I could see from the little crack in my windows, and from the Japanese news over the radio. I had no plan then, as I had no plan later. Plans are of no use in an unpredictable world. Always I lived from day to day, meeting emergencies as they arose. I decided that if the Japanese came in and found me I would hop into bed and pretend to be sick as a dog and stone deaf. Several times they knocked and kicked at the door downstairs, but as the ground floor really was vacant, they concluded that the whole house was empty.

When I was not peering out of the window or crouching over the radio, tuned so low there was only a thread of sound, I sat in the back room and taught myself to type on a small machine I had bought some time before with a vague idea that someday it might prove to be useful. And it did — but that was later on. I read every book in the place, even technical books of my husbands of which I could not make head or tail. But it was something to do. It kept me from thinking. When it grew too dark to see — of course, I could not turn on the lights — I went to bed. After dark I never even opened the door of the refrigerator because of the electric bulb inside. Years later it occurred to me I could have unscrewed it.

Those ten weeks that I lived with Japanese all around the house, sleeping on the sidewalk out in front, going and coming, made me something of an authority on their behavior. Whether I liked it or not, I was never sure that I would not be an accidental witness while some Son of Heaven took his bath under the hydrant in the yard. They would strip for their shower, launder their clothes and hang them on a fence, then bathe and chatter like mad. Their complete disregard of any sanitary facilities was another feature of their encampment in my yard which was anything but pleasant.

Lee and the radio kept me sane those weeks. Lee was a Chinese who had worked for us for years — for my husband and my son and me. Now, with my son in America and Jack in Bataan, Lee felt responsible for me. Day after day, he slipped up to see me, to make sure I was all right and to shake his head dolefully over my unreasonable behavior.

"Miss Peggy, I tell you true I scare," he would tell me. But he always came back.

In some ways, the nights were worse than the days. The Japanese soldiers slept right under my windows and there was one who coughed night after night. I lay there in the dark listening to him, and wondered if he had a family, if his wife was as worried about him as I was Jack.

And the weeks crept on with no news of the outside world but the radio. Hidden in the tunnel of Corregidor was a radio station called "The Voice of Freedom". All the time that terrible siege was going on, it talked to the people. At first, the broadcasts were cheerful. They were all confident that "the sky would be black with planes" coming to rescue the men fighting and dying on Bataan. But they hoped on waited in vain. Not a single plane ever left the ground from those airfields of which the Philippines had been so proud. I myself saw rows of them, smashed and twisted, some still uncrated, some as they stood waiting to take off.

Jack had gone to Bataan. Over and over in my mind the different possibilities turned and turned. Maybe he was there, fighting. He could not get word to me. I knew that. Maybe — and so it would go on, day in and day out. And at night I dreamed of him; he was always climbing the stairs, coming up to me, but he never got there.

Bataan fell. But Corregidor would hold out. Help was on its way. And then the impossible happened. I'll never forget that day in May when the last broadcast came from the "Voice of Freedom." "The men of Corregidor have fought a gallant fight," the announcer said. "Here they expected to come to a little rest. They found a seared and burning hell. Here they fought on and on, expecting the help which never came. Now they must surrender, leaving their dead. ..."

I kept wondering: Does that mean Jack? Could he have gone there from Bataan? Had he escaped? Was he in the hills? Had they taken him prisoner? I thought so hard that I missed some of the broadcast. But I did hear the last few sentences, which were the saddest words I had ever heard.

"... and General Wainwright will meet with the Japanese Military High Command at any place they name, will be in a small launch, carrying a white flag."

Then silence. A white flag. I kept remembering his tall, thin figure on the dock. I had heard how the little boats had taken MacArthur off to continue the fight from Australia. I knew what General Wainwright had tried to do. I knew that he had fought with guns that were obsolete. Now the Japanese were taking him. The words "a small launch carrying a white flag" rang in my ears. It was too bitter for tears.

I looked around the apartment and knew what had to be done. I was going to Bataan to look for Jack.

Isn't It Dangerous

The Japanese were no longer making such a business of stopping people on the street to look at their passes. By this time they took it for granted that all the "enemy aliens" had been rounded up and interned. Now was my chance to get out of my apartment.

As soon as it was dark, I slipped out of the house. I knew I was taking a big risk but I figured that if I kept away from the main streets and the lights, and was lucky in avoiding drunken soldiers, I ought to be all right. My plan was to go to the Malate Convent and see Father Lalor, the gentle priest who was to help me so much and who was burned to death by the Japanese for his efforts. If anyone in Manila could help me, I knew that he was the man.

I had first met Father Lalor and the other priests at the Malate Convent in 1941. A school belonging to the convent had been turned over to the Red Cross to be used as a clinic and I had been assigned to work there. Not in the beginning, however; I always seemed to start things the hard way. I was assigned to work in a hospital which was a long distance from my home. At that time, shortly after Pearl Harbor, another nurse occupied the first floor of the building in which I lived. One night there was a series of heavy, dull reverberations and the windows rattled. I did not know what had happened, but the nurse downstairs had lived in Russia and China. She knew a bomb when she heard it and we ran at top speed for the hospital, in case we were needed.

There was a blackout, of course, and we got lost. At length we came to a graveyard. It was a thick circular wall into which coffins were pushed. (Later we set up our radio receiving set there.) The other nurse and I raced wildly ahead, and it wasn't until we had made a couple of trips that I recognized a white fence and yelled, "Hey, we're running around in circles."

After that, the hospital assigned me to the Malate Convent, which was easier for me to reach.

It was late that night when I slipped inside the church and then out into the convent garden. The church itself was some seven hundred years old, of Spanish architecture, while the convent itself was much more modern. The beautiful garden of the Malate Convent had always seemed to me one of the loveliest spots I knew, but that night its blessed peace was like a little island of refuge in the raging sea that Manila had become.

Father Kelly was thunderstruck when he saw me and he exclaimed, "Look who's running around loose! Where have you been?"

"Hiding," I replied.

"But you can't do that."

"But I am doing it," I pointed out. "Now tell me what has happened."

Father Lalor joined us and they told me that the British and Americans had been put in internment camps, most of them at Santo Tomas; that Greeks and Egyptians were allowed to go around the city if they wore armbands. A few Americans were still free, if they were under a doctor's care and were certified as unable to survive internment, but they had to wear red armbands on the street and they were confined to the city limits.

"But why haven't you been interned?" I asked.

"Because we are all Irish," Father Kelly explained.

"I don't intend to be interned," I said. "So what can I do about it?"

Father Lalor said that if I could wangle a medical certificate I could stay out of Santo Tomas. But that would not do. In the first place, they would get me sooner or later. In the second place, a medical certificate would keep me confined to Manila and I intended to go to Bataan.

"How?" demanded Father Lalor.

"Well," I considered, "maybe I can dye my hair and stain my skin and go as a Filipina."

"And what will you do about your nose?" he asked. I had not thought of that. The Filipino nose is flat and has no bridge.

Father Lalor shook his head. "No American can get to Bataan," he said.

So I went home to think. If I was not going to spend the rest of the war cowering in that apartment, I had to do something about it. If I couldn't be an American, I'd be something else. My husband had a big atlas and I took it down and studied it, trying to figure out what nationality I dared to assume. Jack's name gave me a clue. He came from Virginia, but generations ago the Utinsky family had emigrated from one of the Baltic states. And there was Lithuania, which did not have a consul in Manila, so there would be no inconvenient record of Lithuanian citizens.

Good, I would be a Lithuanian. The only city whose name I could pronounce was Kovno, so that became my birthplace. Peggy did not have a Baltic sound to me, so I changed my name to Rosena. And there Rosena Utinsky, spinster nurse from Kovno, Lithuania, was born, and I began to sketch out the rough outlines of my past life, knowing I could fill in the details as I needed them.

First, I had to account for the fact that I spoke English and that I would not know a word of Lithuanian if I heard it. That was easy. I could fill in with a little truth, which is always convenient, though not essential. For though I was born in St. Louis, Missouri, I spent my childhood on a wheat farm in Canada. Therefore, Rosena Utinsky had been brought as a baby to Canada where she had grown up.

As Rosena Utinsky came to life, all traces of Mrs. John Utinsky, American citizen, had to disappear, so I went painstakingly through the apartment, tearing all names out of books, destroying every scrap of identification I could find, and rolling up family papers in a compact bundle which I could hide or destroy if it were necessary.

The next night I risked another visit to the Malate Convent. "I am a Lithuanian," I told them. "Now how do I prove it?"

Father Lalor explained that I would have to get a residence pass at the City Hall. Everyone had to have one in order to move freely about the city. Of course, he warned me, I would have to arrange for its issuance through some Filipino, as only a Filipino could do it without arousing suspicion. The pass would then have to be signed and countersigned by Japanese officials.

I remembered that before my husband had gone back on active Army duty, we had had a Filipino chauffeur, named Brehada, who was an accomplished penman. I found him, with Lee's help, and for twenty-five pesos, $12.50, he agreed to forge a certificate for me, and he got the proper Japanese signature for it. I still have that pass.

Now at last I was free to come and go without fear in Manila, and the next step was to get a pass which would enable me to get out of the city and go to Bataan. The Red Cross was now functioning as a Filipino organization, under the direction of the Japanese. An expedition of Filipino doctors and nurses was to be sent to Bataan on a scouting trip, to look into conditions and arrange to set up emergency hospitals and clinics for civilian relief work.

The obvious thing was to wangle my way into that Red Cross unit. With all the wounds and sickness and suffering, it did seem that all anyone should have to do was to say, "Here I am; take me." But it did not work out that way. I went from one person to another, begging to be introduced to anybody who could get me into that Red Cross unit. But in those days it was a hard matter to get anyone to vouch for his neighbor — or even for his friend. It was not selfishness. People were just being careful. They had to be. When they knew that all about them might be those who were capable of betraying them, it was understandable enough. And now that I had become a Lithuanian, people were wary of me. No one knew whom I was for or against. In fact, no one knew that about anyone. We were all afraid of each other.

One day I went to see an American woman whom I knew. She was acquainted with my husband and with my son. She was free because her husband, Max Kummer, was a German. If it had not been for Elizabeth Kummer, none of the work our group did could have been accomplished. If it had not been for her, I would not be telling this story now. What she did for me was her way of doing her bit for the Allies. She and Max could not work openly; they did their job through me.

Max had been a German consul in Manila, though he had never been a Nazi. Indeed, he was regarded as a man without a country and he was under a cloud, so far as his own people were concerned. At one time he had been president of the German Club, but he was thrown out of office because he was not regarded as a Nazi; later he was even forbidden to enter the place. But, as a German, he was allowed to keep his radio and after I destroyed my own, along with my American identity, his wife constantly kept me informed of what was happening. She never told me outright, "I heard this over the radio," but every scrap of information she gave me was correct, and time and again, as I got organized, she was able to warn me in time about people who were in danger.

I marched in and showed Elizabeth my pass. "I am a Lithuanian," I told her coolly, and she took it in her stride. "This pass will get me all over Manila but now I want to get out. I want to go to Bataan and find Jack."

"What is your plan?" she asked.

I told her about the Red Cross expedition to Bataan. As I was now the citizen of a neutral country, there was no reason why the Japanese should object to my joining the unit as a nurse. But I did not know how to go about it. I could not find anyone who would vouch for me with the Red Cross.

"I know the man," Elizabeth Kummer said. "Come back in a few days."

Now that I had time on my hands and the freedom of the city I did one thing I'd been longing to do for ten weeks. Early one morning I waited until the American newspaper woman hurried past my apartment and I followed her. She went into the building where the Japanese were printing their newspaper and stayed there for an hour. Then she came out and went to the hospital where she was helping as a volunteer. Well, well, I thought. Another collaborationist!

A few days later I returned to see Mrs. Kummer, who told me that arrangements had been made for me to go to Fort Santiago to talk to the Japanese High Command, under whose surveillance all travel in the Philippines fell. I didn't like it. The idea of talking to the Japanese scared me silly, but I was willing to try it. I'd have talked to Hirohito himself if it had been necessary to get that pass.

But, after all, it was not necessary. Mrs. Kummer did not like the idea of that interview any better than I did. If the papers could be obtained without a personal interview, she said, so much the better. You are always apt to slip up on some detail in conversation, and as we would both have to lie to the top of our bent, it was better not to take chances.

She telephoned to Fort Santiago and asked most respectfully for the staff member in charge of travel. There was a long delay, to impress her with the importance of the speaker, and at length someone condescended to listen.

Elizabeth identified herself carefully, giving him time to check her answers. Then came the real test. "There is a friend with me," she said, "a Lithuanian nurse. Miss Rosena Utinsky." I could almost hear the bespectacled clerk turning the pages as he tried to check that one. "She wishes to go into Bataan to help in the work of Filipino relief." There was a lot of chatter at the other end of the line.

"Yes," she said tactfully, "but you are such a busy man, with so much to do, and so many important things to decide. I wondered whether I might not take her to the doctors in charge of the work."

I could hear the satisfied hissings of the minor clerk who had been called a busy man with important work to do. The flattery worked. She got the permission for me and we were both so relieved we could hardly speak. The longer I could stay away from the Japs, the better I liked it.

The next step was to persuade the Filipino doctors connected with the Red Cross that it was safe to accept my services. She took me to Dr. Sison, in charge of the Filipino relief work, and introduced me as Miss Utinsky. It is a queer thing, but from that time on I actually began to believe my own story. Dr. Sison was in desperate need of experienced graduate nurses and he passed me on to Dr. Thomas Gann, head of the Institute of Hygiene in Manila, who was to lead the Red Cross unit into Bataan.

When I actually held in my hand the papers that meant the High Command had given me permission to go to Bataan, I was ready to believe in miracles.

Within three days I was on my way to Bataan. The purpose of the expedition, as I said before, was to make a survey for the best location for emergency hospitals for the native population, whose "liberation" by the Japanese had left them in hideous conditions, with the ill lying in the fields and along the roads, dysentery victims everywhere, women having babies without help.

We left Manila in a station wagon, four Filipino doctors, five Filipino nurses and myself. We were constantly stopped and challenged by the Japanese, and the Filipinos were terrified though, as a matter of fact, I was the only one whose papers were not perfectly in order. I still remember the Filipino doctors standing stiffly at attention, holding their hats over their hearts, and the nurses frantically making the sign of the cross.

We came at last to the road where the March of Death had taken place. We came so soon after the surrender that the dead bodies were everywhere. There was no evidence that a battle had taken place, yet thousands had died here. Bodies lay all around, some beside the road, some in the rice paddies, some in the ditches. I was sick with shock. I could not believe my eyes.

Every foot of the way brought new horrors. I cannot blot out the awful picture of starved dogs tearing at those poor bodies, running off, growling, carrying a man's hand or a whole arm, tearing at his face. The bodies had been stripped of everything of value, even shoes and identification tags. Japanese soldiers were walking around with American wrist watches strapped on their arms all the way from the wrist to the elbow.

At Abucay there was a bombed church with part of the roof intact, and we decided to put a clinic there. The natives swarmed around us and I asked them why there were so many Americans dead. Then, little by little, they told me the story of the March of Death. For five days and five nights, they said, they had heard the men screaming incessantly. They were beaten with bayonets to make them march faster. They were worn out from the long battle; most of them were sick and almost starved. But they plodded on, some of them dropping right in their tracks. When they fell, the Japanese stabbed them with bayonets and tossed them into ditches beside the road. Sometimes they left the poor emaciated bodies in the road and the oncoming trucks ran over them as they lay there.

I saw a spot where thirty wounded men had been tied together with barbed wire run through their hands, then thrown into a barbed wire entanglement and machine-gunned. Another group of thirteen men were so weak they could not walk. They kept falling. The Japanese wired them together with barbed wire and when one fell he dragged the others down. At length, the Japanese pushed them into an open latrine and forced their comrades, at the point of guns, to bury them alive.

Two Filipinos on that March of Death had cans of sardines hidden in their clothes. They opened them and tried to eat. The Japanese chopped off their arms, flung them into the fields, and then slashed them up, cutting them to pieces. They polluted the water and forced the Americans to drink it. As I walked the roads of the stricken area, I noticed small artesian wells that bubbled up on either side. This explained why so many men in that grim procession lay sprawled in the grotesque attitudes of sudden death just off the roads. They had been mad with thirst and had dared to step aside for a drink of water.

After this trip through filth and nightmare, when everything seemed to be festering death, I knew that I could not stop until I had given every ounce of my strength to help the men who still lived. And somewhere among them was Jack. I felt sure of that. Though I had searched and searched among those pitiful dead bodies, I had not found him.

After what those men had endured, nothing seemed too hard or too dangerous. Now I could not think of the Japanese except as beasts, and every weapon or trick that could be used against them seemed not only legitimate but also compulsory.

Our first job was to work out some plan to stop the rising epidemics that resulted from the March of Death and its litter of unburied dead. The Filipinos were starving too, for the Japanese were as destructive as locusts. The first dead body I saw in Bataan was that of a woman who had been raped to death. In the days that followed we had patients every day, girls from seven years old, who had been raped.

The sight of the living was almost as grim as the pictures of the dead. Wherever I went I found the Filipinos dying by hundreds with dysentery and malaria. We worked feverishly to gather together some help for the stricken people.

We repaired the schoolhouses and made them into crude emergency shelters, carried the sick and dying into bombed churches rather than let them die naked and alone at the roadside.

I saw Filipino families fleeing from the bombed towns, all their pitiful possessions in little carts which the parents pulled in the absence of the horse that had been driven off. Sometimes, laid tenderly on top of the cartload of broken bits of housewares or the last measure of rice, would be the body of a child, carried in this way because there was no time to stop and give the small body decent burial, no church in which to say the prayers for the dead, no priest to give comfort.

Working until I could scarcely stand helped, and it was dangerous work. Truckloads of American prisoners were driven by, the men suffering from malaria and dysentery. I was trying to treat them and see that they got proper drugs when I was stopped by a Japanese officer.

Dr. Gann introduced me at once. "This is Miss Utinsky, a Lithuanian nurse who has volunteered to help us."

He looked at me searchingly. "For a Lithuanian, you speak excellent English."

"You speak English well yourself," I replied, "and you are Japanese."

"Naturally," he said. "I am the Protestant chaplain. I was born in America, and was there for twenty-nine years."

"I grew up in Canada," I told him. "And they speak pretty good English there too."

"You are not to give help to these Americans," he said.

"It isn't because they are Americans," I told him. "But those men have dysentery and malaria. Unless you let us take care of them, they are going to spread dysentery all through the Japanese Army and you are going to have the biggest epidemic you ever heard of. You'll lose more men than you have lost in battle, I promise you that."

Dr. Gann was terrified at my open loss of temper but the Japanese chaplain realized at least that it made sense, so he stopped the trucks that were passing and we filled the pockets of the men with all the drugs they could carry.

My husband and I had lived on "the Rock" at Corregidor so long that some of the boys recognized me. I whispered to Sergeant Don Du Chane that I was a Lithuanian and not to forget it. And I always asked if they had seen Jack. No one had.

One day I found an American flag which had been taken down at the time of the surrender. It was folded under a bunch of papers which looked important, as they described spies who were supposed to be in the vicinity. I gathered up the flag and the papers and wrapped them in a piece of stiff paper almost like cardboard. I hated to leave them behind and yet I had no right to take them with me. If I involved the Red Cross in any difficulty with the Japanese, they would be refused permission to do any more work in Bataan, to say the least of it.

Just before we started back to Manila from the survey, however, Dr. Gann and I went into a church. The altar had been used as a toilet, the heads of the saints had been cut off. In a niche Dr. Gann found a statue of St. Anthony, the only one that had not been defiled. He picked it up.

"I wish," he said wistfully, "I could take this home with me. Then, when the Americans come back, I could return it to the church."

"Why don't you take it?" I said quickly. And I told him about the American flag and the papers. "I won't take them if you say not."

Dr. Gann looked at his St. Anthony, and he hesitated only a minute. "Isn't it dangerous?" he asked.

"They can only cut our heads off once."

He nodded. For some reason, that seemed to make it easier. "Take them along," he told me.

On the way back to Manila some Japanese hailed us and climbed in for a ride. I was scared stiff. I sat clutching the American flag in my arms while a Japanese officer stared speculatively at my white face. He insisted that we all get off to have a drink with him. I didn't dare leave my bundle behind for fear the car would be searched, and I certainly didn't want to take it along. But there I sat, having a drink with the Japanese, while his arm practically rested on that American flag.

When I got back to my apartment in Manila, I washed the flag and hung it up in the living room to dry. My faithful Lee, coming to see whether I had returned safely, took one look at it and nearly passed out. "I scare. Miss Peggy," he said.

But we put the flag away in a tin can and hid it in a far corner of the attic, along with the papers.

The Captain out the Window

It was the last Sunday in May when we returned to Manila. That was the day when the last gallant defenders of Corregidor were marched to Bilibid Prison. Near shore they were pushed off the barges in which they were carried, and forced to drag themselves through the water. Exhausted and starved, wet and dirty from that scramble through the surf, they were marched down the boulevard along San Luis, across the Jones Bridge, and through the gates of Bilibid Prison.

I stood on the sidelines, watching that pitiful march. I saw men fall and saw them kicked and beaten with bayonets. A few Filipinos tried to toss cigarettes to the prisoners and were beaten for it, as were the soldiers who tried to catch the cigarettes. As each tired, staggering man came up, I wondered whether the next would be Jack. I didn't know whether I hoped or feared to see him. I could not have helped him. When I did see boys I knew all they could do was to look at me and lift their hands a little. I could not speak to them. That day it was not easy to pretend not to be an American.

The next day I had my first encounter with the Japanese. Lee and I were in a carromata (a two-wheeled cart) on our way to the post office. All at once two Japanese began to run after us, shouting.

"I guess they want the cart," I told the cochero. "They can have it."

Lee got down and I jumped out of the cart, right beside the Japanese. Without any warning they began to beat me. First they struck me with their fists, knocking me again and again against the wheel of the cart. Then they kicked my shins with their hobnailed boots, dragging the soles of the boots down my legs until the nails had torn almost all the skin off them.

Lee stood helplessly on the sidewalk, looking like death. Anything he could have done would only have made things worse. Then I saw a truckload of American soldiers. They had been stopped and were being forced to watch the beating. That accounted for the attack on me. The Japanese wanted to make them watch me suffer. When I realized what the point was, I made up my mind that I wouldn't cry if they killed me.

For fifteen minutes the beating went on and the American prisoners just looked. There was nothing they could do, nothing they could say.

At last the truck was ordered on and the beating stopped. I was a mess, my body just a pulp of bruises, and my legs torn and bleeding. With Lee's help I climbed back into the waiting carromata. Lee's poor eyes were full of tears. "Oh, Miss Peggy, more better they whip me. More better they whip me."

This was no time to let myself go and say what I felt, so I answered brusquely, "Well, what are we waiting for? Let's go." And we went on to the post office.

Lee had set himself the job of looking after me and it was no cinch. With my husband gone and my son Charles in America, he regarded the problem of my safety as his own special task. He had tried to keep me from going to Bataan. "I very scare," he had told me. And finally, as a last resort he had added, "Miss Peggy, if you get hit with bomb, what I say to Mr. Charley; he no like that at all." I had to laugh.

Then he had put his hand over his heart. "Do you feel — here — you must go?" he demanded. I nodded. So he had nodded his head reluctantly. If that was the case, then I must go.

After that beating, Lee took to slipping into my apartment at night to check up on me. If I hadn't been scared to death already he would have finished the job. I would wake up in the middle of the night, hear cautious footsteps and be sure the Japs were ready to snatch me from my bed. It would be Lee, just looking in to see if I was all right.

"Of course I'm all right," I'd say, "if you wouldn't scare me to death." And he'd go away, shaking his head and muttering his interminable scoldings.

But the pay-off for Lee came when I had to hang the captain out of the window. One night, just before curfew, a Negro woman named Minnie Sanders, whose husband was one of the American prisoners, came to tell me that there was an American officer hiding near her home. He had escaped on the March of Death and made his way to Manila, and he was ill. Someone should look after him. Would I come?

It was impossible to go that night as I could not get back home before curfew and no purpose would be served in getting arrested, so I set out the next morning as soon as curfew was lifted.

He was a Captain Burson, of the 45th Infantry, who had been at Fort McKinley. He was ill with malaria and dysentery and was also shell-shocked. As this was his second tour of duty in the Philippines he knew Manila well, and he had managed to get rid of his uniform and to hide. He had, however, hung on to his Army .45 and all his papers, which were practically an order for execution if they were found.

He was terrified when I walked in on him and denied that he was an American, refused to trust me and did not want to go with me.

There was no time to argue so I just said, "Oh, shut up!"

He was so surprised that he stopped protesting and shook his head. "You are little but you sure are tough," he commented.

He looked so sick and weak that I did not know how I was going to get him to my apartment. "Do you think you can walk a few blocks?" I asked.

He thought he could and while he got ready, I wrapped up the service revolver and his papers in a package and tucked them under my arm. It was a risk but I didn't know what else to do with them, and it was safer to carry the thing boldly than try to hide it. We started down the street in a wavering sort of way, for the man was so weak he could hardly keep on his feet.

"Where are we going?" he asked me, half in fear, half in suspicion.

"To my apartment," I explained. "You need care and I am a nurse. When we get there, I'll send for a doctor whom I can trust."

When I had returned from my trip to Bataan, I began to worry about that vacant apartment under mine. It had been a godsend while I was hiding but now it was a risk. The Japanese might take it into their heads to move into it. I thought it would be safer to have someone there whom I could trust. I heard of a Spanish woman whose sister was interned at Santo Tomas and whose brother had worked for the American Express. The priests at the Malate Convent assured me that she could be relied on so I got in touch with her and offered to pay the rent if she would take the apartment. She could not speak English but her little boy served as interpreter and she was delighted with the idea.

That morning, as soon as I had got the American captain into my apartment and in bed, I went downstairs. Through the little boy I explained to Mrs. Carnesa, the Spanish woman, that I was hiding an American prisoner in my apartment, that he was desperately ill and needed care. I told her that it was a risk and if he were found there, we would all be sent to prison, to put it mildly. I would not endanger her if she was afraid. She smiled, spoke to her little boy and he said, "My mother says to keep the American. She will help you with him."

I sent for Dr. Gann, who examined Captain Burson, gave him some injections and left orders for further treatment. As the days passed, he began to recover, though he was still very weak. Then Lee came on one of his unheralded visits, took one look at the American sitting in a chair and almost dropped dead. For a minute his jaw just waggled; he couldn't get out a word. Then he really exploded.

"I tell you true. Miss Peggy, I scare. Japanese find this American here. They chop off heads."

"They won't find him," I said. "Anyhow, we have to get this man well. And here he stays until he is able to move."

Time passed and there was peace and quiet in the apartment. I should have known that it was too good to last. During one of Lee's visits, as luck would have it, there was a heavy banging on the door downstairs. The Japs had come. Lee blanched. "Miss Peggy, they cut oft heads."

"Of course they will," I snapped, "if we stand here like idiots and don't do something. Help me hide the captain."

My little kitchenette had a window which opened out on the one-story roof of a setback room downstairs. With Lee's help we hoisted the captain out of the window so that he clung to a gas pipe with his toes touching the galvanized iron roof below. I knew we'd have to get rid of the Japs in a hurry. If Captain Burson's hands got numb, he would drop on that iron roof with a clatter that would arouse the whole Imperial Army.

I ran back into the living room and started for the stairs to find out what the Japs wanted. And there, on the table, was the captain's gun! "Here," I said to Lee, "take this up to the attic. You get in through the hole in the bathroom ceiling. Hide it and then run across the roof and stay next door."

Lee didn't move. He stood looking at me. He did not dare obey me and leave me alone. He did not dare disobey me. He just stood, holding that gun in his hands. I was frantic. Then at last he turned and went out and I went to the window. The Japanese stood beside a truck, talking to a Filipino in the street. They had made a mistake. They had wanted the same number on the next street. They climbed into the truck and went off.

It was just as well. I sat down on a chair, too weak to move, and just then Lee marched in, still holding the gun. He put it down with great dignity, his face stiff with disapproval. "I tell you. Miss Peggy," he said, "I very scare. I go now." And out he marched, oozing indignation from every pore.

And there was the captain, still hanging out of the window. I ran out to the kitchenette to help him back in. I tugged and tugged. I was weak from fright and he from illness, and try as I would I couldn't seem to pull him up. At last I hoisted him far enough so that he could catch hold of the sill.

Then one last hard pull and my hands slipped off his clothing. I went reeling back against a little table and smashed all the dishes and the captain sprawled across the sill, breathless.

The Japs had gone this time but I knew that sooner or later they would come again, so that night I locked the captain in the apartment and went out searching for a safer hiding place for him. There was a Filipino whom I could trust. He got a carromata, we loaded Captain Burson in it, and took him several miles away to a kind Filipino family who agreed to give him refuge. The next day I found him a little apartment in a Filipino house.

Remembering those ten weeks I had spent shut up in my apartment, I decided to take a chance of getting a residence pass forged for him so he would be free to move around Manila. He was dark enough to pass for a mestizo, so my forger friend got him papers describing him as an English mestizo.

The rest of Captain Burson's story I learned after my second return from Bataan. Lee told me. The Japanese had found him and had taken him to Fort Santiago for "questioning." After his release I saw him. His right arm was partially paralyzed, his left kneecap broken; he had been chained up by the wrists and then dropped to his knees on the stone floor. His nostrils were burned so badly that in some places only the thin skin remained. They had shoved lighted cigarettes and cigars up his nose while he was hanging, to make him talk. But he didn't talk and at length they let him go.

He sent word to me not to try to see him again; it would be too big a risk. However, I managed to get food and medicine to him, enough, at least, to keep him alive. A human being's will to live is very strong. In a few months the captain was strong enough to go around the streets, doing menial jobs as a mestizo laborer, living in the most horrible quarters, never staying anywhere for long. And this story, like so many others, does not have a happy ending. The Japanese captured him again and this time they killed him in Fort Santiago.

A second Red Cross expedition was being sent to Bataan and, of course, I wanted to go. There was work to be done there, far more work than there were people to do it, and a chance that I could make some contact with the American prisoners. This time Dr. Gann was to remain behind in Manila, and the relief mission was to be handled by Dr. Romeo Atienza. Dr. Gann met with the group before our departure to explain what had to be done and to be sure that everyone understood just what he and she was getting into. And then I had a bad moment.

"You know," Dr. Gann remarked, "several people have told me about some white woman being pulled out of a carromata and beaten badly by the Japanese. A truckload of American soldiers saw the whole affair."

I acted very surprised. No, I had never heard of the case. Rumors were always going around but I paid little attention to them. It was hard to look Dr. Gann blandly in the eyes because I could hardly resist the impulse to look down and see whether the scars on my legs still showed through my stockings. I dared not let the Red Cross get any hint that I was the woman. If they suspected for a moment that anything had happened to me or was likely to happen to me, they would never dare to take me along.

There were more bad moments on that trip. One of the mestiza nurses, Doris Robinson, knew me and sat next to me in the truck as we started for Bataan.

"Where is your husband?" she whispered. "I am Miss Utinsky," I said quickly. "I understand," she said, and never again referred to him.

This time the trip was less like a journey through hell. We hastily set up tents for our living quarters — sleeping quarters, actually, for we were so frantically busy that we never had time to enter them except to sleep. That crowded tent-living led to the next bad moment when I undressed the first night to go to bed.

"For heaven's sake," exclaimed one of the nurses, "what happened to your back?"

"I stumbled and fell down the stairs," I answered, turning around hastily.

"Those are the first stairs," she remarked, "that ever made scars shaped like cartwheels."

I maintained a dignified silence. It seemed to be the only reply I could make.

There was so much work to do that we simply had to do the impossible every day. We took over a bombed school at Caligaman. It was filthy beyond description. For weeks people had been lying there, the sick, the dying, the dead. They had slept and eaten and defecated there. And that was where we must establish a hospital by nightfall.

I drove people like an avenging fury. We carried out the people, swept, cleaned, disinfected, built bamboo cots and by dark we had our patients in it, a functioning hospital.

There was so much to do and so few of us to do it. Dr. Romeo Atienza and his wife, who had come along to supervise the meals, were fine people and I learned within two days that they were staunchly pro-American when he told me that he hoped to find a place to work where he could establish contact with the American prisoners and help them. The Red Cross, of course, was supposed to be giving assistance only to the Filipinos. Certainly, the Red Cross need not have feared that the rest of their doctors would help any Americans; they did not exert themselves to help anyone. With the exception of Dr. Atienza they were not even physicians, just dentists who were not prepared to be of much use, and who sat around most of the time playing mahjong.

And meantime there were wounds to dress, babies to deliver, dysentery and malaria to treat, the starving to feed, the homeless to shelter. For the Japanese had left the countryside stripped of the essentials of living. We had nothing but partly destroyed buildings and bamboo cots and primitive methods, but at least lives were being saved and the hungry and naked were being cared for. The most difficult thing was to stop the spread of epidemics. The dead from the March of Death still lay by the road, up and down which I passed day after day, and flies from that death route were carrying disease everywhere. We seemed to be covered with flies and there was nothing we could do about it.

So far as the American prisoners were concerned, I seemed to be as far from establishing contact with them in Bataan as I had been in Manila. If I stuck to the hospitals we had set up, I never would see any Americans, so I applied for the job of field nurse. There was only one privilege granted the prisoners on Bataan. Every few days, several of them would be allowed to leave their prison and go foraging for a little rice or carabao meat, and they could stay out until five o'clock without risking a beating. If I was going to find them, I'd have to be out in the field.

Dr. Atienza did not like it. "The job is too hard," he said. "You won't be able to stand it. Do you know what the work entails? You'd be stationed one day at Santa Lucia, the next day at Abucay. You'd have up to 200 cases a day at the clinics, and when that work was done you'd have to go from house to house, checking the needs of the population."

"Try me anyhow," I begged, and Dr. Atienza agreed readily enough. After all, someone had to do the work and if I was asking for it —

So I opened a clinic in Abucay to reduce the press of cases at other points and so that we could give the badly needed care as quickly as possible. Those people were living at just about the lowest possible level, with the flimsiest shelters for homes, with subsistence food, with no medical care.

And I plunged in. But I didn't forget that my main object was the Americans and whenever I heard a truck rumbling by, I would look out.

And then came the red-letter day. I was walking along the road when a truck came along. I jumped into the ditch and looked carefully but I saw no one but an American soldier at the wheel. Soldier? He looked like a baby to me, he was so pitifully young.

"Any bedbugs around?" I asked. That was the usual term applied to Japs when prisoners were able to talk to each other and wanted to keep their reference to their captors private.

He shook his head, too surprised to speak. The sight of a white woman, and an American woman, walking around free was more than he could take in.

"Where are you from?" I asked, meaning, of course, which prison.

"I'm from Arkansas," the boy drawled.

I had been on my way to the Red Cross tent and the boy stopped the truck there. His name, he told me, was Marvin Ivy, and he was eighteen years old — and one month, he added, feeling the extra month lent him dignity. Lt. Colonel John Shock and Captain Andrew Rader were in the tent now, trying to get medicine and supplies for the sick prisoners. They had been out since early morning but no one would take the risk of giving them any supplies.

I marched boldly into the tent where the two American officers were talking with the members of the Filipino Red Cross.

"Hello, captain," I said casually.

Captain Rader looked at me for a moment, swallowed, and then answered as though it were the most natural thing in the world for us to meet there, "Oh, hello."

The two men looked half starved and broken in spirit. "When you've finished your talk," I said, "I'll bring your soup."

They pushed back their chairs. "It looks like we're finished here," Captain Rader said bitterly, and the two men followed me out.

I dashed back and heated soup and got crackers, corned beef sandwiches and coffee. They ate ravenously.

"What is the trouble?" I asked.

"We need drugs desperately. The men are sick and they aren't getting any care."

"I'll get them for you," I promised. "You wait here."

While they ate, I collected sulfa drugs for dysentery, 8000 Brewer's yeast tablets, nearly a case of soup, five pounds of cocoa and crackers. They didn't ask where I got them. I explained that I alternated between Santa Lucia and Abucay. "When you see the Red Cross flag, I'll be there."

They told me that Colonel James Duckworth, who had done two men's work in the hospital during those terrible days on Bataan, was ill, but he had sent them out to beg for drugs. In a few days he would send three more men.

"See if you can bring me a complete list of the prisoners, will you?" I asked. "Those who have died, those who are ill, all of them."

They promised that they would try, and I felt that I had taken my first concrete step. At least, I had made contact with the Americans.

Unfortunately, the Red Cross official who had been in the tent with the American officers when I sailed in also knew about that contact. The next morning he was off for Manila and when he came back he brought another man with him who came looking for me at once. I knew then that Dr. Canute had turned me in for helping the Americans and that I was to be sent back.

"I had better pack up my bits and pieces," I told Doris Robinson. And then I got mad with myself for being defeated so easily.

The man from Manila turned out to be rather nice. "Been working hard?" he asked me.

"We all have," I said shortly.

"I am sorry but I have to take you back to Manila."

"Do you always do what you have to do?"

He smiled. "Nearly always."

"Not this time," I told him. "I was never hired by the Red Cross so they cannot fire me. I volunteered. If the Red Cross doesn't want me, the natives do. I have taken care of a lot of them. Not one would refuse to take me in." The more I thought about it the madder I got. "Off the record, who turned me in?"

"Dr. Canute —for aiding American prisoners."

"Of course," I said cautiously, "I'm not an American, as you know. But after all, these boys came out to fight for the Filipinos. And yet if anyone wants to give them a few drugs to keep them alive, you want him removed. You go back and tell Dr. Canute I won't leave Bataan until I am damned good and ready and that will be when there's not another American left here."

Well, he shook hands with me and he went back to Manila and resigned from the Red Cross.

A few days later I was working at the clinic when I saw three American soldiers. I ran out to meet them. As I expected, they were the three men sent by Colonel Duckworth: Captain Jack Le Mire, Neil Burr and Charles Osborne. They had brought me the lists of the dead and the prisoners. Jack's name wasn't there. But I had made another start — that of collecting such lists. The day was to come when I had the most complete lists of anyone in existence, and they helped the War Department to trace men who had simply dropped into oblivion.

"We are being sent to Camp O'Donnell," the men told me.

Somewhere they had been given some boiled duck eggs and some warm beer. I rounded out the feast with crackers and jam and we sat there eating and drinking and laughing as though we hadn't a worry in the world, though if a Jap had come along just then there would have been a mass beheading. We knew it and still we laughed.

This time I really loaded them up with drugs, food, twenty-five pound boxes of prunes, and so forth.

"Where in the name of God did you get this?" they exclaimed.

While we were talking. Captain Le Mire pointed. "See those hills?" he asked. "There are a lot of guerrillas fighting over there."

"Let's go," I said.

"Well, it would be a shame to leave these groceries."

Of course, the reason the Japanese permitted these men to leave the prison on foraging trips was because they figured that they would have no chance to escape. And the Americans did not make the effort because they believed it was a pointless risk. MacArthur had said he would be back, and they expected him to arrive at any time. That was one reason, I suppose, we endured all we did. We didn't see ahead. At first we lived from week to week, awaiting the return of MacArthur. After that, when the whole game got more dangerous, we lived from day to day; and those last months, just from minute to minute.

When the Americans left I called after them, "Goodbye, I'll see you at Camp O'Donnell."

And that night I came down with dysentery. There was a tropical deluge, I remember, and nineteen times I pulled on a coat and staggered out in the rain to the primitive toilet.

Next morning Dr. Atienza looked at me in horror. I was so weak I had to hold on to the cots while I looked after the patients.

"It's this night life," I snapped at the doctor; but my condition frightened him.

"You white people can't take it," he declared.

"The hell we can't," I retorted. "Look at the rest of them," and I indicated the beds. "At least, I'm still on my feet."

But I wasn't for long. I lay in that tent, covered with swarms of flies, getting sicker and sicker. The natives heard about it. There was a woman whose little boy I had nursed with pneumonia and she sent a two-wheeled bamboo cart, hauled by a carabao and nursed me for four days. I lay there wracked by nausea, falling into a doze, coming out of it to more sickness. The Filipina woman picked tender leaves from a guava tree and gave them to me to chew as a help against the disease, but I was too weak to chew them.

One day I heard the sound of marching feet and drew my head up so that I could see out. It was my men, marching out of Bataan to Camp O'Donnell. I lay there, crying weakly.

Now my work in Bataan was done and I was as determined to get out as I had been to get in. But Dr. Canute, who had tried to have me removed, now refused to take me out. The nurses went to him and said that I would die if I were not taken to Manila for care. Dr. Canute was not interested. "There's no way to get her there," he said.

He came to see me and I pointed out, "You have a truck. You could drive me back."

He yawned. "I'm too tired," he said.

"You'll get me to Manila or I'll write to the Governor of Bataan. He's a friend of mine. If I die, he will see that my letter goes to the Red Cross in the United States and people will know what goes on here."

He took me back. At every bridge, of course, we crossed Japanese lines, but I was too sick to care this time. When he left me at St. Luke's Hospital in Manila he said, "You understand, the Red Cross is not responsible for any expenses Miss Utinsky may incur." That night Miss Wiser, Superintendent of St. Luke's Hospital, Nurse Ross and Dr. Forres worked over me, and the next morning Dr. L. Z. Fletcher, who was interned in Santo Tomas but was permitted to call at the hospital each day, came to me.

Those weeks in the hospital were literally a nightmare. After the first shock of seeing the line of the March of Death I had thought that I was accustomed to its horrors. But now, in my delirium, I dreamed constantly of it. And always, in my dream, those tragic dead were stirring, were trying to come back to life. I could not bear it. I would scream to them not to get up and have it happen to them all over again. They were dead; they must not try to fight again.

There was only one bright spot when a rumor reached me that Jack was in Bilibid Prison. It was the first time I had heard anything of his whereabouts. But the next day Captain L. B. Sartin, a naval officer, got word to me that while it was true Jack had been there for one night, he had been moved and no one knew where he had been taken. But they did know that he had been captured on Corregidor, in the tunnel which he had helped to build.

At last I was strong enough so that I could stand up if I had something to hold onto and I left the hospital. There was not a carromata in sight and I started to walk to my apartment. Walking was something I hadn't bargained for, and I could take only a few steps without toppling over. Along the street there were high iron fences and I held on with both hands, pulling myself step by step until I reached a comer, when I would wait until someone came along and helped me across.

Finally I knew I could not go any farther without rest and a glass of water and I knocked at the door of some Spanish friends I knew. I knocked and knocked and finally the man came to the door. He didn't say anything. He just looked at me.

"Let me come in," I said impatiently. "I'm ill. I'm just out of the hospital. I must rest and have some water."

Still he stood there, looking very queer. I almost pushed my way past him. "Where's your wife?" I asked.

"She's — out." He made no move to get me the water, just looked at me. I knew he wished I hadn't come. Then I saw he was looking yellow, staring out of the window. Two Japanese were coming up to the house.

"Out!" he said. "This way." And he pushed me toward the back of the house.

I went along the corridor at a sort of shambling run and fell against a door. It opened and his wife stood there, looking at me, as her husband had done, without speaking.

"How do I get out?" I asked frantically. "There are some Japs at the door."

She showed me the way, told me how to circle the house and come out on another street and I got away, half walking, half crawling.

When I finally got home I was so exhausted it was all I could do to get into bed. I had no energy left to wonder about the queer behavior of my Spanish friends.

I had to get back my strength quickly for I was to take a private case the next day, a job which Mrs. Kummer had got for me. It was an American named Van Vorries, vice president of General Motors, who had kept out of internment camp because he was very ill.

Every morning Lee came for me with a carromata. He would push from behind and the cochero would pull and between them they got me into the cart and out the same way. I could barely stand and how I looked after Mr. Van Vorries I don't know. Between my looking after him and his looking after me, we both got well.

It was while I was nursing him that I mentioned casually the puzzling behavior of my Spanish friends. He inquired about it and we discovered what had happened.

Just a short time before I had knocked at the door, a young American girl had come to call on my friends. She was out of Santo Tomas on a pass. She was followed by two Japanese, who forced their way into the house and, while one of them kept my friends in the living room at the point of a gun, the other one took the girl into the kitchen and raped her. The girl was still in the house and the Japs had left only ten minutes before my arrival. The girl, as it developed, contracted a venereal disease. My Spanish friends complained to the Japanese authorities, who told them that the guilty man would be executed. Later, when the American girl was returned to Santo Tomas, she saw the man acting as guard. He grinned widely as he recognized her.

I was well again and I remembered my promise to the boys, "I will see you at Camp O'Donnell."

Then a letter came from Dr. Atienza. "Our people need you," it said. I knew what it meant. He had found a way of establishing contact with the American prisoners at Camp O'Donnell. The next day I was on a train going to Capas.

"Miss U"

When the Americans were rounded up after the surrender of Corregidor, the Japanese began to release their Filipino prisoners. The Red Cross was on hand for each release date, to look after the Filipinos and to bring those who were ill back to Manila in cattle cars.

Dr. Romeo Atienza, the Filipino doctor with whom I had worked on that second relief expedition to Bataan, had managed to establish himself at Capas, near Camp O'Donnell, and to make contact with the American prisoners, so I was all set to join the Red Cross nurses at Capas, my excuse being that I was on my way to help the Filipinos who were being liberated.

I did not know yet what kind of arrangements Dr. Atienza had made, but there must be some way of getting supplies into Camp O'Donnell. There had to be. Now at last I had found a use for the provisions with which I had stacked my apartment just before the fall of Manila. At least the food from the American commissary was going to feed Americans.

So that first trip of mine to Capas had all the earmarks of a minor evacuation. I filled sack after sack with groceries. I even stacked a trunk full of them. By the time my packing was done, there was a mountain of bundles which, somehow or other, I had to get to Capas.

Then came the labor of getting carts. The cochero lost enthusiasm when he took a look at the trunk, but by dint of persuasion, threats, and the flourishing of a few pesos, I finally got myself, my trunk, and my assortment of sacks, bags and bundles to the train.

By one of those paradoxical chances that come up in wartime, I found a redcap, rushing around the platform among shouting and gesticulating travelers, crying children who had lost their parents, and scattered baggage. I collared him and though he was dismayed at the prospect of getting all my loot stowed away on the crowded train, he didn't have a chance to get away from me.

He decided the easiest way would be to shove the stuff in through the window, so I climbed on, pushed my way to a window, and pulled the sacks in while the redcap pushed from outside. I shoved the stuff anywhere, under my seat, under every seat in reach, while the Filipino passengers gaped and even the calm Indians watched me, their dark faces kindled with interest.

At length everything was safely on board except for the trunk. I called, "Take that to the baggage car," and then raced through the train to make sure the trunk actually came aboard. The cochero edged his cart down the length of the train, the red cap heaved and I tugged, and the trunk came aboard just as the shriek of the whistles sounded. The train was on its way and so, thank God, was I.

The trunk was safe but there was no telling about the bags and bundles. I knew my travelers in Philippine railroad coaches, so I hurried back through the train to my seat. A perfect barrage of questions greeted me, so I explained that I was a Lithuanian nurse on my way to Capas in Tarlac province, where I was going to look after the Filipino prisoners who were being released by the Japanese. Many of them were sick, all of them were hungry.

The Filipinos nodded their heads. Yes, they agreed, it was true. There was much sickness and hunger these days. And with their curiosity appeased, they retired to their own seats, pushing aside children, squawking chickens, and whatever livestock they might be transporting with them. The train settled down to its journey and so did I.

By the time the train was whistling for Capas, I had begun the Manila process in reverse. Capas was a whistle stop and I had to get my stuff off quickly or not at all. I enlisted the help of everyone in reach and got them to promise to put my things out of the window as soon as the train stopped. Then I ran back to the baggage car to look after my trunk.

I found it all right. Sitting on top of it was a fat Japanese.

Even if I had known how to talk to him, I would not have been able to at that moment. I just grunted and pointed to the trunk. He looked me over, saw my Red Cross band. Then he grunted. He pointed at me and then at the trunk.

"You, you?" he asked.

I nodded my head nearly off.

He pointed at about everything in the car and asked, "You, you?" I could have gone off with the whole carload of stuff. He pushed the heavy trunk off on the platform, grinning and hissing.

On the platform I found a cochero. While the Filipinos were poking things out of the window, the cochero reached over the barbed wire that ran along the tracks, hauling my baggage over the wire, loading it frantically into the carretela (two-wheeled box-shaped cart); then he rushed from window to window, catching the last of the bundles just as the train began to lurch on its way.

Dr. Atienza, his wife, and some Filipino nurses were living in a little house which a teacher had turned over to the Red Cross. It did double duty as residence and Red Cross headquarters. A guest was no problem as there was no furniture and everybody slept on the floor anyhow.

The carretela, creaking under its load, drew up before the little house and Dr. Atienza looked out of the window and then rushed to the door.

"Miss Utinsky!" he exclaimed. "What on earth did you bring?"

"You said you needed things," I told him, "and I brought some along."

He shook his head in disbelief. "I knew you would come," he said, "but not in such a big way," and we got busy unloading the cart.

How great the need of the American prisoners was I did not learn until I had talked to Dr. Atienza. As a member of the Filipino Red Cross he was permitted to visit Camp O'Donnell, where he was allowed to look after the sick Filipino prisoners. They were not, of course, supposed to have any contact with the Americans or to give them any aid. But Dr. Atienza had managed to get in touch with Colonel Duckworth, Major Berry, and Chaplain Tiffany, inside the prison, and through them he was confident that he could get help to the Americans.

Our men, he said, were starving. The Japanese allowed a pittance to the soldiers, ten centavos (about five cents) a day, with which they had to buy their food. Officers were given twenty pesos (about ten dollars) a month. With the permission of the Japanese, the officers had pooled their money so as to provide food for all. But even this amount was cut, as a man was not paid if he was too sick or too weak from lack of food to work.

The men desperately needed food, money to buy food, drugs, clothing — and all of this would have to be smuggled in. But Dr. Atienza had discovered a way to do it. When the Filipino prisoners were released, those who were ill were brought out of the prison in ambulances or trucks to be loaded on cattle cars. These ambulances were carefully searched when they left the prison, lest someone should try to escape or blankets should be smuggled out, but no search was made when they returned to the prison.

We could hardly have asked for a better arrangement, since this meant that Dr. Atienza would be able to take in the supplies I had brought with me without any danger of having them confiscated.

Next morning, as he was preparing to pack my supplies in the ambulance, he asked suddenly, "Why don't you send in a note with these things, asking for a receipt? In that way, you may be sure that your supplies are actually reaching the American prisoners."

I agreed and wrote the note. Then I hesitated. I did not know how to sign it. If it were found, there would be trouble for everyone, and trouble in a big way for me. So after a moment's thought, I signed the note "Miss U." And with that signature, the Miss U organization came to hazy birth.

From that time on, all sorts of stories and rumors circulated about Miss U. I listened to all kinds of speculations about myself. I was Chinese. I was Russian. I was everything under the sun.

That day. Dr. Atienza came back from Camp O'Donnell bringing a receipt for the stuff I had sent in. Well, at least we knew where we stood. Dr. Atienza could smuggle the stuff in if I could get it. I knew that as long as my commissary supplies lasted, I would have food to bring them. The problem was clothing, drugs, and money.

I arranged with Dr. Atienza to go up to Capas for each release date, when Filipino prisoners were sent back to Manila. I began traveling back and forth to Capas like a commuter, each time loaded with all the food I could carry, but all I could carry was terribly little for so many men in desperate need. It did amuse me, though, to think that I was carrying it all on a Japanese railroad. There was a certain justice in that.

But food was not enough. The men needed drugs. They needed clothing. And most of all they needed money.

In any conquered city, one commodity is prized above all else — money. And I needed it badly. I went back to Manila after that first trip and looked around the apartment to find what I could sell. Before the war, my husband and I had been proud of our silver service, and of our Spode and Wedgewood china, but now it had nothing for me but a cash value. I sold the china for over $200 and the silver for $400. My rings and pearls and a bracelet, sold to a jeweler, added a lot more money to my supply. There was nothing else but my electric stove, and I heard of a couple at the opposite end of Manila who were trying to furnish a house. They were so glad to get a stove they did not quibble over my $200 price. One by one, the possessions that had given meaning to my pre-war life were passing from me, but at least I was accumulating a sizable sum with which to buy drugs and clothing for starving men.

Buy as carefully as I could, however, the money dwindled away, just as the food cache, which had seemed so inexhaustible when I had first filled the apartment, shrank smaller and smaller.

Well, if I could not buy, I could beg. I went to Father Lalor with my problems and he helped me, as he was always to help me. Day after day he walked the streets of Manila, asking everyone he could trust for old shoes. Between the two of us, we must have collected several thousand pairs, which we stored at the convent until I could get them to Camp O'Donnell.

I became a regular panhandler. I begged everywhere. In shops, in churches, in the houses of friends, in the offices of total strangers. Getting clothing and drugs and food, I told them in the beginning, for the Filipinos. There was so much to be done that I could not handle it alone, and there was always the risk of asking the wrong person for help. But I figured that unless I took risks I would get nothing done.

So I went to the people I knew best, to those I knew were loyal to the United States, and told them bluntly of the urgent and dire need of the sick and starving men at Camp O'Donnell.

They were afraid. Well, I could understand that. Live under enemy occupation long enough and you begin to breathe an air of suspicion. You don't trust your friends or your neighbors or your own relatives. And most of the time you are probably justified. But part of the hesitancy of my friends was as much for my sake as for their own. I understood that too. Not simply because they feared I would be caught by the Japanese, but because they thought I might become involved with some unscrupulous group that would be vile enough to exploit even the unfortunates in the prison camps.

"How do you know, after all," they demanded, "that the things actually reach the prisoners?"

"That's easy," I explained. "Everything that I send in has a note with it, asking for a receipt. If you get a receipt, will you believe that you have really made contact with the American prisoners? Will you help them then?"

Yes, they would believe if they got a receipt.

So I went back to Capas again and with Dr. Atienza's help smuggled the money from my furnishings and jewelry into the camp, part of it going to Chaplain Tiffany, the rest to Colonel Duckworth for the hospital. I asked the men to send out notes indicating what they had received, and telling me what they needed. Then, armed with the prisoners' notes, I went back to Manila again.

The notes turned the trick. Through Father Lalor, I was able to reach American sympathizers — Chinese, Swiss, Spanish, Filipino — whom I tapped ruthlessly, though few of them knew my identity. To most of those who helped me, except those who became a close part of the organization, I remained "Miss U," a woman whom nobody knew.

Notes from the prisoners were shown to anyone from whom we could beg a few pesos, or order food, or medical supplies. Soon the life-saving stuff was coming in to us in an ever increasing stream. We stored it at the convent until it could be delivered. And night after night, when I had gone to bed, I allowed myself to wonder whether any of the food was reaching Jack. I had not heard a word, yet somehow I knew he was a prisoner somewhere. Risks did not seem too dangerous when I thought of him inside those fences.

America, in the summer of 1942, was faced with a grave lack of quinine, but in Manila it was still being sold by the Swiss and Chinese drug houses which, oddly enough, had not been closed. Sulfa drugs were also on sale, as was the triple vaccine used for dysentery, typhoid and cholera. I mobilized my friends to join me in buying small quantities at a time to build up a stock.

Medicine was, of course, the most difficult product to smuggle, but we did it by emptying half a sack of beans, putting the drugs in, refilling the sack again and giving it a special, but almost indistinguishable mark which indicated to our contact inside the prison. Sergeant Gaston, that it was to go to the hospital.

Again, through Father Lalor, I obtained the help of the Maryknoll sisters who were nurses and who worked with a will for the American prisoners. From a closed hospital they salvaged thousands of pajamas which we cut up, making each into two pairs of pants and a polo shirt. In the beginning, they were cut in three sizes, small, medium, and large. Toward the end, we made only one size — small.

One night I had gone to the home of Ethel and Ernest Heise to pick up some of the pajamas on which they were working. It was late when I left but I managed to get a carromata and climbed in with my big bundle of pajamas. The driver ignored my instructions, which called for following dark streets, and turned into a wide, lighted one. The headlights of an automobile fell on my white face, lighting it up, and some Japanese in a carromata between the automobile and me caught sight of me.

The cochero turned and said stupidly, "Those Japs are drunk."

"I know," I told him. "Go fast!"

He blinked at me and let the horse plod on. The Japanese meanwhile had turned around and were whipping their horse.

"Go fast," I said frantically. "Hurry!" I got out my door-key, slipped the strap of the bundle over my arm and was ready to leap out. The other carromata was gaining on us. The driver stopped at my door. Thank heaven, my street was dark and the great palm tree in the yard threw a deep shadow.

I threw the cochero his money, leaped out of the cart into the shadow of the palm, and plunged the key straight into the lock, a thing I'd never been able to do before at the first aim. The Japanese were going too fast to stop and passed the house.

I ran up the stairs, locking the gate, bolting my own door, and then, with my knees sagging, I peered out of the window, not daring to turn on the light. The Japanese had jumped out of their carromata now and they were running up and down the street, shouting, screaming with anger, hunting for me in the shadows.

Just then two Russian women turned the corner and came down the street. The drunken Japanese grabbed them and dragged them away. I was so scared that I went to bed.

There was enough horror in Manila without going in search of it, but with the other Americans locked up, in prison camp or internment camp, I felt that I had to know what was going on, that I had to see it for myself so there would be someone to make a record for the days when the Yanks would come back.

The worst of all the prison camps was Camp Nichols, outside of Manila. I punished myself by going there, but I had to know. Here I hid upstairs in a native house, overlooking the prison, and saw things so grim that it is hard to believe today that they happened.

There I saw five Filipinos, four men and a woman, beheaded one after another. There I saw two Americans stripped naked and hung on a mango tree. And late one afternoon I saw two American prisoners carrying in a third man. I could look down on his face from the window where I crouched. His ribs had been caved in, his whole torso was a mass of bruises and open bleeding wounds. There was blood gushing from his mouth and nose and I knew that he was dying.

The two Americans carried the wounded man up some steps and out of my sight. Then I heard the sound of blows and screams. But the screams did not come from the man they were beating. They came from the enraged

Japanese. Then in a little while the man's body fell sprawling limply off the steps and some American prisoners ran down the steps, grabbed up the body and took it around the building, where it was buried.

Later I learned what had happened. Sidney O. Await wrote to me saying the Americans were working as slave labor in groups of four, on an airstrip. They were filling boxcars with gravel and rocks — all by hand. Then four more would push the car down to another four who unloaded it. The men had to do ten cars a day on a diet of lugao and what they called pumpkin soup.

This man was so weak that he fell. The Japanese began to kick him but his strength was exhausted and he could not get up. They kicked him in his ribs and nearly killed him. Then his comrades carried him in, where I saw him.

The Japanese carried blackjacks and for no reason at all they would hit a man. After the prisoners had brought the man in, one of the Japanese, called the Wolf, stood him against the wall, took a hose, put it in his mouth and turned on the water. The prisoner did not struggle, he was dying and too weak to do anything. The other Japanese, called Cherry Blossom, took the blackjack and hit him over the head and then let him fall to the ground. The names of those Japanese I later turned over to the Army. I hope they have not forgotten them.

Smuggling Is A Full-Time Job

On one of my regular trips to Capas, I walked into the Red Cross room as usual and there sat a small Japanese. Since the Red Cross was working under Japanese direction — or at most with their permission — such visits were to be expected, but they never failed to startle me.

As I came in, the little man pointed at me and began to scream, "American! American!"

Dr. Atienza raced up in alarm and protested, "No, no, not American, Lithuanian. That is like German — friends to you."

The Japanese looked unconvinced and Dr. Atienza touched my uniform. "Look," he said persuasively, "Kangafu Lithuanian, Kangafu."

"Oh," said the Japanese, "How you say Kangafu in German?"

That stumped me. The only German word I had ever heard was deutsch. But it was a start, so I might as well use it. "You say nursie, deutsche nursie," I told him, and the Japanese turned away satisfied, smiling and hissing.

As soon as I got to Manila, I went to see Mrs. Kummer and asked her to tell me the German word for nurse so I would be prepared. But I never had a chance to use my information. The next time I went to Capas I saw my same little Japanese and with him was the biggest son of Nippon I had ever encountered. They both stood looking at me. Then the big one began to roar, "American! American!"

That was a signal for the little fellow to assert his superiority. "No," he expostulated, "not American. Nursie, deutsche nursie."

Dr. Atienza had to leave the room in a hurry to conceal his laughter. The big Japanese glowered at me for a moment and then went on.

Both Dr. Atienza and I realized that sooner or later someone was bound to discover my American nationality in a way that I could not disprove. It was fantastic luck that, after having lived in the Philippines so long, someone had not already recognized me and given me away to the enemy. We tried our best to avoid unnecessary risks that would endanger the whole enterprise. But there was one risk I did take, and that was in meeting three American prisoners. Captain James Kelly ran the light plant in Capas for the Japanese, with the help of two enlisted men. At night the men would slip across to Dr. Atienza's house, one or two at a time, and there they would give me information as to what was actually happening in the prison camp. Though they slept at the plant, they went in and out of O'Donnell every day.

Later, when they were moved to Cabanatuan, their successors, Captain Hix Meir and Vernon Booth, were able to keep up the flow of information. You must remember that these men had to do the jobs they did; they were literally slaves. To refuse would simply have cost them their heads. That would have happened, of course, if they had been caught giving us information.

One day I was talking with two of these Americans when Dr. Atienza ran up. "Go into the station right away," he said. "There's a Jap slapping women around and he is coming this way. I'll go the front way and get your ticket; you go through the path past the tent."

I went. The men dared not go on with me. I took off right down the track and with speed. Then I looked around. Running after me as fast as his bandy legs would carry him was a bigger than average Japanese. He had a long black mustache and his teeth were showing, his lips stretched by the effort of running.

Right ahead of me was the Americans' tent. I dared not go in, for it would have cost them their lives to protect the object of a Japanese chase. I turned around the corner of the tent like a breeze and kept going on down the path. The Japanese thought I had gone inside and stopped to see. That saved me.

The only thing I could think of as I was running was the story of the little Negro boy who prayed as he ran from the bear, "Oh, Lord, help me! But if you can't help me, Lord, please don't help the bear."

I reached the station and leaped up on the steps of the last car just as the train pulled out. Dr. Atienza came tearing out of the station with the tickets, which I snatched from his hand. It wasn't much of a train but it looked good to me. After I was safe, I was so weak I could hardly sit up. How I wished I could go to bed!

Later, the men in the tent told me they had never prayed so hard in their lives. I guess the Lord heard them, for something gave me the courage to stay out of that tent and run for the train.

When I went back to Capas on the next trip, Dr. Atienza called, "How's my Olympic runner today?" But he added that he had never spent a worse few minutes.

Dr. Atienza told me that he had complained to Colonel Ito, the Japanese in command of the section, and that he had assured him that such a thing would not happen again. Nurses were scarce and they were needed. Dr. Atienza told them that I was a volunteer who worked without pay. Apparently they really did discipline that Japanese. The next time I saw him, he was a pretty battered looking specimen. But I wasted no pity on him. If I had not been so scared that I fairly flew, I would have been the one who looked that way.

Before long the task became too heavy for one person. I could not carry enough supplies at one time to be of sufficient use, and those constant trips, loaded down with bundles, were becoming too conspicuous. I needed helpers, and they appeared just at the time when I needed them most: Naomi Flores and Evangeline Neibert, who dressed as Filipina vendors, with a cloth tied about their heads, could go bargaining for supplies even in Capas itself without arousing suspicion.

Naomi Flores was an Igorote girl, reared and schooled by an American family in Baguio, the mountain province. Less than five feet tall, quick and smiling, she had been a successful beauty operator in a shop whose owner had been interned. One day Naomi came to see me and said that she had overheard me talking in the shop, begging for clothing for the Filipinos who were being released. She asked whether she could help me with my work, wrapping packages and things like that. She proved to be so helpful, resourceful and trustworthy that she soon became my right hand man.

I discovered before long that she did not have enough money to live on so I asked her to move in with me. She brought along some of her beauty equipment, a permanent waving machine, dryers, manicure outfits, which later, as the organization expanded, were useful to us in establishing a reason for people coming and going at the apartment. When we began to have code name, for the protection of the people who helped us, Naomi was called Looter.

Somewhere Naomi heard of two Americans, Barney and Tommy Lassa, who had escaped from the March of Death and were hiding in Manila. I suggested that she put them in the empty beauty shop until we could figure where to send them. In the meantime we would at least be able to feed them and no one ever entered the deserted shop. So Naomi smuggled the Americans into the beauty parlor and put up cots in a booth for them.

A few nights later, I came back from Capas, bringing with me some receipts from the prisoners. At that time, I never took any incriminating evidence home, knowing the apartment might be searched at any time, so I went to turn them over to Mr. Nailor, an Englishman who was not interned because he held Filipino citizenship.

Before I could speak, he asked, "Have you been home? Have you seen Lee? He is looking for you."

"What is wrong?"

"I don't know. He said he would go to the station to meet you."

I exploded. Lee knew better than to meet me at the station. He was not supposed to be seen with me anywhere at any time. If I was ever caught, it would be the end of Lee.

I went back to my apartment at once, and Mrs. Camesa, who lived downstairs, called her son, greatly excited. He interpreted for her and told me that the Japanese had come to the house three times. I went upstairs and, as was my invariable custom when badly frightened, I went straight to bed.

It was not long before I heard Lee slip into the apartment. "Oh, Miss Peggy," he lamented, "I very scare."

So was I and that made me madder than ever. "You'll be worse scared if you don't tell me what happened."

Well, it was bad enough. A Spanish woman who lived near the beauty parlor had looked out from an upstairs window and caught sight of the American boys in the beauty parlor. She had promptly turned them in to the Japanese. Now the Japanese were looking for Naomi.

There was just one thing to do — bluff it out. I had to find Naomi before the Japs did and convince her that she must beat them to the draw. Go to them before they got to her, ask what they wanted, tell them she had hired the boys — whom she took for mestizos — to guard the shop.

Naomi agreed. If she was afraid — and she must have been, for all of us were scared to death most of the time — she did not say so. The next morning, of her own accord, she went to Fort Santiago. That was a horribly long day. I kept imagining what had happened to Naomi. What had possessed me to think of such a plan? And suppose she talked! That would be the end of me. It would be the end of the food and drugs that kept Americans alive at Camp O'Donnell.

It was seven o'clock that evening before Naomi came in. I knew at the first glance our bluff had worked. The Japanese, she reported breathlessly, had questioned her for hours. And they had slapped her only once. That was because she said that she had gone to the shop two or three times;

later, she answered the same question by saying, "a couple of times." They did not know what she meant.

That questioning was useful, however. Naomi told the Japanese that after the owner of the beauty shop had been interned and the place was closed, she had taken some of the equipment to my apartment where she was continuing her work. But it was not the end of the episode.

The next day, I remember, was a Sunday. There was a knock at the door and when Naomi opened it, two Japanese walked in. They were two of the men who had questioned her at Fort Santiago. If there is one thing in which I have been lucky, it is in the people with whom I have worked. Naomi did not turn a hair. She stuck to the pose of friendliness she had adopted as her role at Fort Santiago, introduced the Japanese as two friends, and went out to make tea.

They drank it with polite noises and asked casual social questions. And one of them, seeing an atlas on the table, opened it and pointed to a map of the world.

He swept his hand over the Western Hemisphere. "This," he said, "is for Japan — this for Germany." He disposed of Europe to their ally, kept Asia for themselves. "That is the way it will be after the war. Where will you live then?"

I considered the matter. "In Manila, I think. Lithuania will probably be destroyed."

They bowed their way out but they had not missed anything. When the Japanese finally caught up with me, they had a record of every casual remark I had made that afternoon. Fortunately, I have a good memory.

As time went on, we set up a regular banking business to get money for the soldiers. The prisoners themselves helped in these money-making schemes. An organization inside the camp co-operated with the smugglers outside to receive pesos, distribute them where they would do the most good, and acknowledge receipt of all moneys received.

Some of the officers, who had been stationed in Manila, still had accounts in the banks there, and Manila people cashed checks for them to the amount of hundreds of badly needed pesos, while loans were floated on personal notes payable six months after release. Where the prisoners had no checks, they wrote on dirty, torn scraps of paper which were honored without hesitation. At first we smuggled in large denominations, but that proved to be too dangerous and after that we sent one-peso notes. On five cents a day, an enlisted man had no business with anything over a single peso. Even so, the Japanese marveled at the thrift of the Americans who, paid almost nothing, managed to have money to buy fruit and beans.

When I read General Wainwright's moving story, I was reminded that some of the burned money which he mentioned once came into my hands. While the bills were burning, some of them were blown away before they were entirely consumed. The men picked up the pieces and later one fifty-peso bill, a couple of twenties, and several tens and fives were sent out to me. I inquired of Mr. Byron Ford, manager of the Philippine Trust Company, who was interned in Santo Tomas, whether such bills were redeemable and was told that they were if enough of the serial numbers was left to identify them. That was another break for some of the boys. I got the bills cashed and sent the money back in to them.

So the work went on. Naomi finally moved out of my apartment and went to Capas to live, pretending to be related to one of the families there. She was in a better position to make contact with the prisoners, and she became a distributing and contact agent there.

Evangeline Neibert, whom we called Sassie Susie, was the daughter of a former member of the Bureau of Education who had owned a large plantation, an American married to a mestiza school teacher. She was well educated and she had some nurse's training. Sweet and infectiously gay, Sassie Susie was like a little Irish colleen. Her sweetheart was an American, soldier in Cabanatuan Prison. She would dare anything and narrowly escaped capture several times. When the boy she loved was sent to Japan, she just dug in harder than ever.

We had fallen into a routine now. We collected money and supplies in Manila. We packed them, hiding the money and notes and drugs. We stored supplies at the Malate Convent. From the contact people in Capas to the contact people in the prison camp, messages and supplies must be taken and lists brought back out. Day in, day out, the game went on.

We would try anything. A short-sighted lieutenant wrote anxiously on a small dirty scrap of paper to say that his glasses had been broken when a Japanese sentry struck him in the face. Could Miss U, he wanted to know, figure a way to get them repaired? I did and after that there were a lot of requests from men whose glasses had been broken during the beatings to which they were subjected. They would save the pieces, smuggle them out to me and I would take them into Manila. One of the prisoners was a Major Willard H. Waterous, who had had an optical shop in Manila. Joining the Army after Pearl Harbor, he had later been in the hospital at Bataan when it was bombed. He was captured, but his office force still functioned and the glasses of the prisoners were mended there. Only one doctor, a Spaniard named Sabater, ever demanded money for this work.

"All right, I'll pay for them," I told him.

Then he put the glasses into an envelope, with no protective covering, and to add insult to injury, reached for his advertising card to enclose.

"Never mind the card, doctor," I said. "I won't forget you. Neither will the Army."

One prisoner, Captain Sidney E. Seid, wrote to me saying he hoped I would not think he was crazy. But I seemed to be able to get anything into the prison. Could I possibly get him some oil paints to help while away the deadly prison hours? I did, too.

It was curious, at a time when life was stripped down to fundamentals, and the whole thing cut to a problem of keeping alive, that the hunger for art in one form or another remained as pressing, as acute as it did. Several times I encountered men whose longing for music became almost an obsession, so that their dreams were filled with it.

As the weeks wore on, more and more thank-you notes were smuggled out. When my helpers had nothing else to do, I set them to writing to some of the boys whose names we had learned from the lists sent out to us, and they served an incalculable part as morale builders. Whenever one of these boys mentioned his date of birth, we made a point of doing something about it. And the response was enough to break our hearts.

"Dear Miss U," one of the boys wrote. "Before I start to write this note, I want you to forgive me for my clumsy writing. I am writing this just at daybreak as we are leaving camp. They say we are going to Japan. When I opened your note and saw my birthday card, tears came to my eyes. I shall be indebted to you for the rest of my life for your kindness. I just can't say how I feel at this moment. My heart is full of joy that people can be so kind to me.

"I can't say more; we are getting ready to leave.

'GOD BLESS YOU. Your friend,

Edward Mike"

Other notes like this came from Sergeant Robert Underwood, Sergeant Edward Smack, Sergeant Henry Vara, Sergeant A. L. Lawrence, Sergeant John Henry Poncio. Lieutenant Arnold W. Thompson, of their outfit, asked each man to write a note of thanks to Miss U. Some had sent out checks which I was able to cash.

One afternoon I was coming back from Capas to Manila with Naomi and Evangeline. Before we reached Manila a typhoon struck so violently that the train would hardly continue against it. Water poured in everywhere. When we got off at the station in Manila, the wind was still howling, and the rain coming down in a deluge.

As it happened, the blouse of my uniform was stuffed with documents, notes from General L. B. Stevens, Colonel Duckworth and Chaplain Tiffany, receipts from the men. Some of the boys had had the good luck to get some belated Government warrants.

I got off the train first and the girls, according to a system we had followed from the beginning, kept their distance. We never appeared to be traveling together.

A squad of Japanese soldiers was standing at the gate with drawn bayonets. I did not like it at all but I walked forward slowly. Promptly three Japanese fell in on either side of me, two in front, and two behind. Out of the corner of my eye I saw Salome Holland (her husband had died a few months earlier at O'Donnell), who had come to the station to bring me cash for a check I had given her the day before, move away unconcernedly without another glance at me. The Japanese could hardly have picked me up at a time when I had more damning evidence on me, and the worst of it was that it implicated so many of the prisoners as well. My armed escort wheeled and turned into a room at the left of the station. Here there were more uniformed men. All I could see, in my terror, was that, compared with the Japanese, they were enormous. "My God," I thought, "the Germans have landed."

Then I heard an unmistakably American voice say, "Now, perhaps we'll get some action."

My escorts and I halted with military precision ten paces outside the door. A tall American began to talk and a queer thing happened. I was so terrified at being surrounded by the Japanese with their drawn bayonets, my blouse filled with incriminating evidence, that I was stone deaf. The girls, who had followed at a discreet distance, said later I was so white they could not tell where my uniform ended and my skin began. I saw the American's lips opening and I could not hear a sound.

Then all of a sudden, as though water had run out of my ears, I heard the screaming of the typhoon, the downpour of rain, the whistles and noises of the station.

"I'm sorry," I said. "For a moment I could not hear you. Will you tell me again?"

The American officer explained that he was Major C. C. Heinrich. One of the men with him was Colonel John P. Horran, another Captain Allan Crosby. I did not get the names of the others. They were prisoners who were being brought down from the mountain province of Baguio in a truck. On the way, guerrilla forces had attacked and killed six Japanese sentries. Now they were being taken to Cabanatuan prison camp by train and for two hours they had been waiting for someone who could speak English.

At last, as I understood the situation, I began to function normally. That armed escort with drawn bayonets was just the simple way in which the Japanese had picked out an interpreter.

"My wife and children are in Santo Tomas," Heinrich explained. "I have been trying to tell these soldiers that all I ask is to call my wife and tell her that I am alive, that I am here. Do you know any officer you could ask?"

I wrote down the request and indicated my Red Cross band. A Japanese soldier took the paper and went away. While we waited for him to return, Captain Crosby asked me whether I could locate his brother for him and get word to him of his whereabouts.

The Japanese came back and nodded to the telephone. I called Santo Tomas and got in touch with Mr. Bert Holland, who was a monitor, and arranged correspondence and calls for the internees. He said that Mrs. Heinrich and her children were at Holy Cross Convent and if I called a bit later he would let me know what could be done.

I sent out for coffee and food, which the men needed badly, and when I telephoned again I was able to tell Major Heinrich that his wife and children were on their way to have a short visit with him before he was sent on to Cabanatuan.

The typhoon was still raging when I left the station. At a safe distance, Mrs. Salome Holland was waiting for me. I gave her all the money I had. "Spend what you need for food and coffee for these men on the train," I told her. "Get it to them somehow."

Mrs. Holland nodded and set off. She got packages of food and jars of hot coffee and bought a ticket for Caloocan, the next stop on the train that was to carry the Americans to prison. On the train she found a reliable Filipino, who promised to get the food to the men.

Before leaving the Americans I told the men, "You'll hear from me again." It worked very well. Mrs. Heinrich was able to keep in touch with her husband, and Crosby's brother managed to send money to him. So all in all it was a good hour's work.

Then, at four o'clock on a December morning, when I was at Capas, I was awakened by singing.

"Good-night, ladies. Good-night, ladies," drifted back to me. I knew. The prisoners were leaving Camp O'Donnell, marching off for Cabanatuan prison camp. They were going out singing.

They sang because they felt sure that whatever lay ahead would be better than what lay behind. How, they reasoned, could it be worse? Only 200 men were leaving Camp O'Donnell. In the prison graveyard lay 1700 of their comrades who could not march with them. They had died since May. Only 200 saved. Somehow, in some way, I would have to operate on a bigger scale at Cabanatuan.

I never saw the men again, but I knew I had to keep working for them and for others like them. And perhaps Jack might be where they were going.

Jack

If I was going to help the prisoners in Cabanatuan prison camp, I would have to find a new method. I could no longer use the excuse of Filipino relief, which had made it possible for me to go and come from Capas, because all the Filipino prisoners had been released.

There was no use attempting to make any plans until we could look over the ground and find out what the situation was, what possibilities for smuggling there might be, and how we could work out some method for making contact with the Americans.

I sent Naomi with two Filipino boys to the little town of Cabanatuan to scout around and see what they could learn. They went as peanut vendors, hawking their peanuts near the prison gates. Naomi was the first of them to make a contact — with Colonel Mack, who was a slave laborer on a vegetable garden project near the camp.

When I first heard of that garden I thought, "At least the men will be fed here. They will have the vegetables they grow. They won't starve." I never was more completely wrong. There were vegetables, all right, but not for the half-starved prisoners who worked in the gardens, loaded vegetables in carts and then took them to the kitchens to be cooked for the Japanese.

One of the first questions Naomi asked Colonel Mack was whether Jack Utinsky was at Cabanatuan. He answered that he was going back into camp and that he would be out again that day. While he was inside, he succeeded in asking a number of men about Jack. When he met Naomi again, he slipped her a letter. "This will tell you what you asked," he said, and he went on with his work.

That night Naomi brought me the letter at the apartment.

"Dear Miss U," it read, "you have many friends in this place. It is from them that I have been able to get this story of your husband. I am deeply sorry that I have to tell you what I found out. Your husband died here on August 6, 1942. He is buried here in the prison graveyard. I know how you have tried in every way to get word about him. I am sure that this is the true story. Men here who knew him verified it.

"You will be told that he died of tuberculosis. That is not true. The men say that he actually died of starvation. A little more food and medicine, which they would not give him here, might have saved him.

"This is terrible news for you, who have, with your unselfish work, been able to save so many others. All of us will always owe you a debt that we can never pay for what you have done.

"I do want to say to you that this place is far more dangerous for your work than Camp O'Donnell was. Do not take risks that you took there. If you never do another thing, you already have done more than any living person to help our men. My sympathy goes out to you in your grief. God bless you in all you do.

"Sincerely yours,

"Edward Mack,

"Lt. Colonel, U. S. Army"

I did not cry. I was too numb for that. Naomi said the comforting things one does say at a time like that but they did not seem to make much sense. I sat there holding the letter. Jack was dead. He had starved to death. If he could have received just a little of the food I had given to others, he might be alive. If I had found him four months sooner, he might be alive.

In one way, it was a relief to know the truth. Every night, until I heard that he was dead, I dreamed of him, always climbing, climbing the stairs, and never reaching me. And during the day, with every atrocity story, with every hideous thing I saw, I wondered, "Is that happening to Jack? Is he being tortured? Is he ill? Is he starving? Where is he? Where? Where?"

Now at least I could remember him without fear, a tall man — six feet — with dark brown curly hair and green eyes. When I last saw him he had weighed 180 pounds. How he must have changed before he died! He had been witty and entertaining, spoke Spanish flawlessly, and eleven dialects as well. He knew the Islands as few Americans knew them.

He had gone to Manila first as a lieutenant in the Army in 1913. During the First World War he was sent to Siberia; and when the war was over he left the Army, after being made a captain, and became a civil engineer in Government service.

It was 1934 when I married him. I had gone out to the Philippines, a young widow, just twenty-six, with a small son. It was to have been a six-month visit but I loved the Islands and the visit had stretched out to seven years by the time Jack and I were married. His work was on Corregidor, the Rock, the impregnable fortress. It was a good life, full of movement and fun and people, with all the easy warmth and gay companionship of Army life in a tropical city.

The first indication that anything would ever change that happy life came in 1940. I had returned to the States to see the New York World's Fair. One morning I was listening to the radio and heard an announcement that the Government would soon order all Navy women to leave the Philippines. That meant the next order would apply to Army women and I had no intention of being shelved somewhere away from Jack, if there was going to be trouble. I headed straight for the Pacific Coast to catch the first boat for Manila.

No women, Army Transportation informed me, would be permitted to go back to the Philippines. The way they said it sounded pretty final. But Major General Walter K. Wilson was in the States and he had been in command at Corregidor. He knew Jack. He wrote to the Quartermaster General in Washington, pointing out that I had lived in the Islands for many years, my home was there, and my husband. So they let me go.

The ship that took me back was a small vessel that had formerly belonged to an Alaskan fishing fleet. The *Etelon* carried 85 Air Corps officers, 428 soldiers, a few nurses, and me. I seem to remember that most of the time aboard ship was spent playing poker, one of my favorite amusements. When the boat docked at Manila, I introduced one of the boys to Jack and he said, "Sir, may I suggest that if you plan to retire soon, you take your wife with you on world cruises. She'll be able to pay the expenses."

Jack laughed. "It's a good idea," he said. "But not yet. We'll wait until we are old."

Then came the order — which I refused to obey — that all American women were to return to the States. Instead I took the little apartment in Manila. Jack was sent to Bataan.

It was at Christmas time that he came back to see whether I was all right. We had two days together, punctuated by bomb blasts.

On December 28, Jack had to go back to Bataan. That day Manila was declared an open city, and as though in mockery, the Japanese poured on the city the worst bombing it had suffered. I was caught in the raid and I think the longest four hours in the history of man was the stretch I spent in an iron chicken coop below Quezon Bridge. I didn't dare get out of it and I expected the bridge to go every minute.

Jack and I had little time together those two days. I was working at top speed at the hospital, and running the canteen, and helping to pick up the pieces from the bombing.

Then Jack had to go back. He stood at the window a long time. At last he turned around. "I came back here," he said slowly, "thinking I'd have to pull you out of a ditch. Instead of that, I found you scurrying around, pulling other people out. I'd like you to know, darling, that I'm very proud of you."

I never saw him and never heard from him again.

The reason that had been the mainspring of my work was gone. But remembering that Jack could have lived if he had had food and medicine, I was determined to go on. It was more important than ever to go on.

So I began to map my new campaign. Naomi was to go to Cabanatuan and work there as a vendor. The second day she rounded up two Filipina women who wanted to help. They lived near the prison gates. Naomi could stay with them, and they would get about and make contacts with the Americans as they went to and from the camp and vegetable farm. The husband of one of these women, an American Negro, was one of the prisoners there.

It seemed like a good start and I made a promise to myself that I would go on with the work until the Yanks came back or until the Japanese caught me.

Our first contact augured well for the work. Lt. Colonel Mack would be able to help us at Cabanatuan as Colonel Duckworth had done at Camp O'Donnell. What had become of Colonel Duckworth I did not know. Word had reached me that all full colonels and generals had been sent to Japan — but not Colonel Duckworth. He was ill, and the Japanese wanted no tuberculosis, dysentery or any men who were unable to work in the land of the Son of Heaven.

The size of the job appalled me. There had been 1700 prisoners at Camp O'Donnell. At Cabanatuan there were more than 9000 men. It was a mountainous task, and if these prisoners were to be kept alive, my operations would have to be speeded up and handled on a far greater scale than I had ever contemplated at O'Donnell. Well, there was no point in being scared before I even got started. The idea was to make a beginning of some sort.

Up to now I had been working on a permit which allowed me to travel back and forth to Capas to help with the Filipino releases. I needed a new kind of permit, "for the needy of Cabanatuan." Mrs. Kummer arranged it for me, and the Japanese interpreted the "needy of Cabanatuan" as the Filipinos of the district, which is what I meant them to do.

At Camp O'Donnell we had smuggled our supplies into the prison in empty trucks and ambulances. The situation at Cabanatuan was different. There was no question of our getting anything into the prison here. As Colonel Mack had pointed out, this was a lot more dangerous than our activities at O'Donnell had been. Our job, therefore, was to contact the Americans when they came out of the prison and get our supplies to them directly.

Every day about a thousand prisoners went out to work on the farm where they raised vegetables for the Japanese. When they came out, the guards would allow them to spend their pay by buying from the native vendors who circulated among them with baskets on their heads. Then, several times a week, the prisoners came out with bullcarts pulled by carabao to buy what vegetables and fruits they could at the stalls.

Of course, before the men could buy anything at the stalls they had to have money, so Naomi and Evangeline Neibert, dressed as vendors, with baskets on their heads, went about with sacks of roasted peanuts. They sold these sacks to the prisoners for a centavo, and in each package of peanuts we hid money, as much as two or three hundred pesos, which was possible because all the money was paper and could be rolled up.

It worked like this. A prisoner would come up to a vendor, buy a sack of peanuts for a peso, get back a ten-peso note as change and a bag of peanuts containing a lot more.

This was not a drop in the bucket compared with the needs of the camp. We had to find a way of getting quantities of food to the men. We needed a truck to ship the stuff in, and we needed some place at Cabanatuan where we could dispose of it to the prisoners without arousing the suspicion of the Japanese, who guarded them every minute. It seemed like a tall order, but we managed it.

One of the Filipino dealers at Cabanatuan was a man named Maluto who had a number of stalls in the market there. One day Naomi stopped to talk to him. To approach anyone and ask for help with our work was the most dangerous thing we had to do. Not only the safety of the individual but also the safety of the group was at stake every time a contact was made. For if we made a mistake and struck a collaborationist, that would be the end.

The Japanese had killed Maluto's son and he was no collaborationist. He was heart and soul for the Americans. But when he looked at Naomi he was not impressed. She wore ragged clothes, with a dirty shawl tied over her head, a typical vendor — which was what she wanted. Probably

Maluto, like many people who think of underground workers and spies as glamorous people, expected something mysterious, a woman who looked like a storybook character.

Seeing his dubious expression, Naomi just laughed. "If you think I look funny," she said, "wait till you see Auntie."

Auntie was the password at the apartment for me at that time. Before long I was so widely known as Miss U that it became my code name.

Maluto was afraid and he didn't pretend otherwise. But he took my address and he came to see Auntie. He listened to my story and he promised to help. Yes, he would let us use his stalls for smuggled goods for the Americans.

Now the problem was to get the supplies. It is curious that our smuggling took the form of one apparently unsolvable problem after another. Almost as soon as a problem arose we found a way of handling it.

Through Lt. Colonel Mack, our first contact inside the prison, we gradually worked out the same system we had used before: notes to the men, receipts for what they had received. The only difference was that we could no longer smuggle the notes in by ambulance or have Dr. Atienza bring them out. Each exchange had to be made with the prisoners themselves as they came and went at slave labor, closely guarded by the Japanese.

The need for food and drugs and clothing and — above all — for money was more desperate than it had been before. The conditions under which the men lived were horrible, they were starving and many of them were hospital cases. To get anything, there had to be money. As time went on, I discovered that people who were hesitant or even indifferent about providing money for unknown men would be most helpful if they knew the person whom they were aiding. There was something real and immediate about the hunger of a particular John Smith; an unidentified soldier was hunger in the abstract.

So I sent word that the prisoners were to give us the names of anyone whom they might know in Manila. Lt. Colonel Mack talked to them and asked them to send me any names they could. "But don't waste time thinking about casual acquaintances," he warned them. "Mind, only those you can trust."

One by one, after that, names would be forwarded to me. I never hesitated in approaching these people. They were both rich and poor, and not one ever failed to give me as much as he or she could in money or food. And never was I betrayed. In all my recruiting of volunteer help, indeed, I never met a single fifth-columnist through people whose names were sent me by prisoners in the camp.

Each time I asked for little in the beginning. "Wait for a receipt," I said, "and then you can be sure that your friend actually received what you sent him." When they got the receipts they began to contribute regularly. Each prisoner so provided for meant that there were fewer to draw on the main kitty. And yet there were still so terribly many!

The garage of the Malate Convent was a convenient storehouse. No suspicion was aroused by loads of supplies leaving there, for the Irish priests had a whole countryside, naked and starving, for which they felt responsible.

After a while I began getting so many supplies that it was no longer possible to carry them piecemeal by train. And again, when the need arose, we found the means to meet it. A wealthy polo player, Juan Elizalde, owner of a distillery, gave me the use of a truck and alcohol to replace gasoline as motor fuel. Elizalde — whom we called Ezy when we began to use code names — was a cultured, thoughtful intellectual, who was well aware of the barbaric implications of Japanese rule and glad to be of use to the organization. He not only contributed the truck but he also gave us everything he could scrape together. Nothing was too much for him to do. Like so many of those who gave us their wholehearted support, he was picked up by the Japanese, and died at Bilibid Prison in the days just before the Americans came back.

Again, as at Camp O'Donnell, the almost childish simplicity of our arrangements was their guarantee of success. Several times a week, our truck went back and forth from the convent to Maluto's stalls at Cabanatuan, and the same system of code messages employed at O'Donnell was used.

With the truck I could send quite large shipments to the camp area. There were no difficulties. Our Filipino drivers were within the law. There was little restriction on their moving about. And doctors and nurses were privileged under Red Cross to give relief. So we were able to keep moving without arousing too much comment. The truck was loaded with sweet potatoes, drugs, canned foods, mongo beans — the latter a superlative preventative and treatment for beriberi.

The day our shipment was made, one of our workers at Cabanatuan would get word to the prisoners that it was coming and describe what we were sending. That day the Americans would present the Japanese commandant with a list of items they wanted to buy in the market. The list always tallied with what we had for them. If I sent in clothes, they said that was what they needed. Obviously this list could not cover more items than might be purchased with the money they obtained from their "Geneva Convention wages." After seeing that the list and the money tallied, the commandant would sign the statement and the Yanks drove their carts off to market.

Of course, they never went to Maluto's stalls first. But after inspecting the vegetables on sale at the other stalls they would come to my friend. There would be a great haggling over price, under the watchful eye of their Japanese guards, then a deal would be made. All of the items on the list would be loaded into the carts. But in addition there would be all the food and medicine that I had sent to Maluto's stalls. Back to camp would go the carts. The first man in the procession would present the list with the commandant's signature. The sentry would examine it. Within half an hour my food and medicine would be doing their job.

What happened, of course, was that everything they "purchased" at Maluto's stalls they really got for free. Then they had their money to buy extra food and perishables that I could not ship them at the other stalls. And always, among the sacks they acquired at Maluto's stalls, there would be one that was marked with red lettering, which was taken to our head contact man in the prison. This sack was filled with pesos and a note indicating which men were to receive the money, and how much was intended for each one. The money would then be distributed inside the prison.

As was inevitable with our activities on so big a scale, the little town of Cabanatuan was aware of the work that was being done. Pretty soon almost everyone in town was either working for me or wanting to work for me. There were a few, of course, who collaborated with the Japanese. That was true everywhere. But we soon learned who they were and so we could be on our guard against them. The other people in town would look after them for us.

Narrow escapes were the order of the day at Cabanatuan. Looter and some of her companions were coming back from the slave labor field where they had ostensibly been selling bananas and peanuts when a truck drew up alongside them. The Japanese driver leaned out and asked Looter to ride with him. She was frightened but she dared not show her fear. After all, as a Filipino, she was one of the "liberated" people. She climbed into the truck and chatted in what she hoped passed for a friendly fashion.

"Mericans very funny," the driver said abruptly. "Don't get much money, all time get little bit, but use it like this," and he made a gesture as though stretching rubber.

Naomi tried to laugh but she was alarmed, wondering whether the Japanese had spotted her activities. The driver let her off in town and she reported to me. The whole thing might merely be a chance encounter and an idle comment, but she took care to avoid trucks after that. If the Americans were to be kept alive — if any of them were to be kept alive under the starvation regime on which the Japanese were keeping them — risks had to be taken.

Sometimes the gratitude of the prisoners took odd forms. One lad went to Chaplain Tiffany, who was one of our chief contacts inside the fence. The chaplain gave him money to buy fruit or peanuts from the vendors when he was out working, but the boy said that was not what he wanted. With his face stiff with embarrassment he said he wanted to write a letter but he didn't write good or spell or such. Would the chaplain help him?

They finally evolved this note, which Captain Tiffany smuggled out to me just as the boy had put it down:

"Dear Miss U, I don't need much money but if some of them Miss U group would write me a letter it would build up my morale."

Another one sent me a poem, the last verse of which went like this:

We're the forgotten men of Bataan,
Maybe some can prove our worth,
And some will tell some strange tale,
Of this horrible Hell on earth.

The Needy of Cabanatuan

By the next spring I had gotten thinner, wiser, and harder. I had never been completely alone, but now there were many who worked with me. I want these people to be remembered. No formal list of citations will ever bear their names. No medals will ever reach them. Yet they are all so much worth remembering.

High on the list of members of the group should come Father Lalor of the Malate Convent, who died a martyr to his creed of love. He was known in the code as Morning Glory. Without the assistance of this holy man and the priests around him the movement could not have become what it was.

Ramon Amosategui, dashing and fearless, an ex-Naval officer of Spain, and then a wealthy property owner, was a dynamo of energy for the group and we named him, appropriately: Sparkplug. He was brilliant and tireless and he did not know what fear was. He reached me through his Spanish wife, who, using the beauty equipment as a cover, came to see me and gave me 200 pesos for Lieutenant Arnold W. Thompson. She waited — rather skeptically, as she confessed later, to see what would happen. Then she got a receipt from the prison. As soon as that arrived, Ramon came in.

Even to meet me was a risk for Ramon and he cautiously arranged the meeting through a one-legged guerrilla, Bert Richey, whom we both knew. He said he could get money from all the Spanish group and he proceeded to do it. Then he took me to a meeting of Swiss residents of Manila and enlisted them as donors. He continued to work for us until he was captured and killed at Bilibid during the days when the Japs were murdering thirty men a day at this prison.

It was Sparkplug who set up a forbidden shortwave radio in the graveyard with its circular wall and took down the broadcasts in shorthand, though he risked the death penalty every time he did it. He brought his notes to the apartment and I typed them. The typed sheets were taken to Cabanatuan, where our distributors got them to the men who took them into camp so the prisoners could learn the truth about what was going on. They called it "The Cheer," and it made them feel that they were part of things again, not just forgotten men rotting in a foul pen. Possession of these news sheets would have meant torture or death, for the Japanese depended upon the propaganda they issued to break the spirits of the Americans.

Known on the code books as Per was an Italian with Filipino citizenship, whose real name was Paravino. He managed to get us a great deal of assistance from other Italians, and he, too, was killed at Bilibid Prison.

From a hospital from which he was never able to leave during the entire period, Ernest Johnson, an officer of the Maritime Commission, rendered a unique service. We called him — and with reason — Brave Heart. Ernest Johnson, shut off from all activity as he was, seemed to be in the center of a web to which he held all the strands. He was associated with the guerrillas in the hills and his hospital room became a meeting place for them. It was through one of them that he first heard of me and he sent for me, asking me to call on him at the hospital. I did so and he offered to help.

He was a man with an infinite number of friends. They came to see him, he would persuade them to donate money and I would give them a code name and see that the receipt went back to Johnson. They never knew who I was; I did not know their real identity. Only Ernest Johnson knew both ends of the puzzle and kept the funds flying. The priests from the Malate Convent would call on him and spend an afternoon talking, drinking rum, exchanging rumors and information that could be passed on where it would be useful.

Ernest Johnson was careful not to take risks. He never sent me a message. That was one thing we all learned. Whenever he had news or money for me, he would send a Filipino boy with a bottle of rum. That was his way of telling me that he wanted to see me.

Through Kurt Gantner, a jolly Swiss, known as Curly Top, I got an even stronger hold on the Swiss colony, which had advantages because it was a neutral group. His wife was called Screwball Number Two; her sister, Marceline Short, wife of a major in Cabanatuan, was Screwball Number One, and Mrs. Amosategui was Screwball Number Three. Each one had a job and did it to the very end, when the Yanks came back. Their code names were silly ones but when you are spending your time in a pretty grim way, it helps to have something to laugh about.

Another family, every member of which worked for us, was the Mencarinis. The husband, Joaquin D., was known as Rocky, his wife, Augustias, as Boots and later as Sunflower, the daughter Elvira as Little Boots, the oldest son Manuel as Hotshot and the youngest one Ralph as Skeezicks.

There were two Russians who did a good job for us. The woman, whom we called Bakala, was married to Walter Jastin, an American civilian in Cabanatuan, whose anxiety had drawn her into the group. The man, Herman Roles, was cashier in a Russian cafe, where he received and sent messages and money. He possessed a remarkable memory and checked nightly on the funds he handled, balancing them to a cent. His code name was Fancypants.

Brother Xavier of the De La Salle College worked under the name of Mr. X. An excellent helper was Scatterbrain, whose husband, an American sailor, died in Cabanatuan. Her real name was Madeline Cripe. One of Dr. Moreta's daughters was known as Cleopatra; a Spanish girl named Solita Cerco signed her notes Sally Brown. Bill Orland was known as Speedy, and Dorothy Claire Fuentes, mother of little Dian — of whom a great deal more later — was called High Pockets.

One steady contributor to the community fund and to a Major Howard Cavender during his imprisonment was Don Vicente Madrigal, a man of great wealth and owner of the Madrigal Steamship Line.

Early in the work at Cabanatuan I met Nati, a lovely Spanish girl who had married an American officer a year before the outbreak of the war. Her husband, Lieutenant Walter Ashborn, had been sent to Bataan and he had managed to get a note to her by a Filipino boy. Nati decided that she would go to him. It took two days, by foot and by banca, but she got to Bataan and met her husband. A kindly CO., Major A. E. McConell, discovering that she had been doing secretarial work, gave her a job and let her stay.

Then word came to surrender. The group to which Lieutenant Ashborn belonged thought they would try to get into Manila by truck. But they met the Japanese instead. They were forced out of the truck, carrying their equipment, beaten and kicked into line and ordered to march. They were struck if they looked back.

Nati watched her husband through her tears as long as she could see the line. She never saw him again so she came to me, knowing I had the most complete lists of the prisoners, and hoping I might have some word of him. I had. Lieutenant Ashborn had died in prison of dysentery and starvation. So Nati rolled up her sleeves and went to work for us.

Our contact men inside the fence had code names too so if any notes were found — and soon enough they were — the identity of the men would not be known to the Japanese. Lieutenant Colonel Edward Mack was called Liver and Chaplain Tiffany was known as Everlasting. Through these two men, by the way, we smuggled out a practically complete roster of the camp, which was later turned over to the War Department to check on the last-known whereabouts of missing soldiers.

And all the time, of course, Elizabeth Rummer helped us in essential ways, which made the functioning of the organization possible, and her husband gave and gave.

There were not, as you can see, very many of them. They represented men, women and children; people of different nationalities, people of different races. They all risked their lives, not once but over and over again, and always deliberately, of their own free choice. They were, I think, pretty swell people.

So it went on. Then it became apparent that even the truckloads of food and drugs were not enough for the camp.

Some way had to be found to increase the amount of provisions that I could get to the men. That way, too, was provided.

Maluto had arranged to rent a boxcar from the Japanese in which he shipped supplies from his Manila warehouses to his stalls in Cabanatuan. I asked him to rent a second boxcar to carry my stuff. At first he was reluctant to do so because he had seen too often what happened to his people when the Japanese chose to retaliate on them. But he finally arranged it.

Whenever I received a message reading, "I am going to visit with my mother," I knew that Maluto was loading his cars in Manila. That was a signal for Sparkplug or Fancypants to go to the Malate Convent, fill the carts with the supplies we had stored there, and drive the carts to the boxcar for unloading. By this fast method of shipment we were even able to send such perishables as green vegetables and fresh fruit which the men needed. All my workers, of course, dressed like Filipinos and they loaded the boxcar without any trouble.

Each large sack of vegetables would contain somewhere in the midst of its contents of red beans or mongo beans or camotes, packages marked with a sign or numeral. Lieutenant Colonel Mack would have lists which had gone ahead by runner with the name of the man for whom the package had been prepared opposite the sign. There was never a slip-up. These packages might contain anything. We answered every single request we humanly could from the prisoners, even having false teeth repaired which had been broken when the Japanese were beating the prisoners.

The amazing part of the thing was that our boxcar traveled up and down on the Japanese railroad right under the noses of Japanese guards in the stations, along the route and at both terminals. Never was there any interference with that enormous flow of food and drugs. It seemed like a far cry from those days at Camp O'Donnell when I traveled to Capas, surrounded by my motley array of bundles, crying Filipino babies, and squawking chickens. Then I had worked practically alone. Now I had more than a score of workers and a smoothly running organization. It was to cost something in pain and in lives, but that was not yet.

At Cabanatuan, the bullcarts would come lumbering out of the prison. The prisoners would go to the stalls to bargain. Maluto was ingenious in the way he handled the supplies. One day he would put his own goods in one stall and mine in an adjoining one. Then he would alternate the stalls or put two stalls of my stuff at one end and his own in the middle two. The work was so dangerous and security so precarious that no worker took any unnecessary chances in these respects.

We got from 30,000 to 40,000 pesos into the camp every month, plus all the supplies the men pretended to buy from Maluto. But even so, with 9,000 men on starvation rations, the best we could do was too little.

One thing that helped was that our supposed vendors were able to mingle with the men doing slave labor on the farm and messages would be exchanged. On a bridge a Filipino boy would be singing a lusty song. A man would drop out of line. Under a bush, hidden under a stone near a bridge, or beneath some leaves in a ditch, would be a package of money. The man would be able to snatch it up and hide it. Naturally, the discovery of such a package would have gone hard with the prisoner, but their need was so desperate that they were more than willing to risk that.

A line of prisoners might find a fat Filipina woman singing as they passed her house. That meant that on the return to camp a prisoner would find a package at the edge of a clearing. When the bullcarts came out on wood detail, an accidental passing on the road would give information that a certain tree held the precious package. When grass had to be cut for the carahao that furnished meat for the Japanese, and the ounce or so a month that the men got, someone would be waiting on the path to give and receive the messages.

We also put both money and messages in match boxes that were carefully concealed in the prisoners' carts. By the end of 1943 we had established smuggling channels wherever we wished. And purchase was not our only method of obtaining supplies. When we could not get what we needed in any other way, we raided storehouses controlled by the Japanese.

While we were busy smuggling to the men at Cabanatuan, we began to smuggle to a small detail of Americans who were still on Corregidor. They were engineers who had been kept there after Wainwright's surrender, probably to keep up various installations.

One night Maria Martinez, one of my workers whom we called Papaya, saw a Filipino boy whom she knew, an engineer on a small launch that plied between Manila and the Rock. He told her about this little group of forgotten Americans. There were less than two hundred of them and they were nearly starved. The Japanese were selling them food at such prices as twelve pesos for a small can of corned beef, and twenty-five or thirty for a large can of sardines.

Papaya brought her friend straight to me and I questioned him closely. He gave me the names of several men he knew there: Captain Keasey, Captain John Lucas, Major Robert B. Lothrop, Major Van Oosten, Captain Pigg. As it happened, I knew all these men and I was sure the Filipino was telling a straight story and was not a spy. Still, I could not afford to take a chance, so I asked him to bring me a list of the men when he returned the next time. When I got hold of the list I felt sure he was telling the truth, as I found on it more names of men I knew. From then on I managed to get food and money to the stranded men.

The most maddening thing of all was that the men who did slave labor on the farm, raising vegetables for the Japanese, were beaten and often killed for taking so much as a bean or a cucumber.

There was one nineteen-year-old boy on a work detail. Like most of the men he was half starved. One day he saw some children and asked them for food. They promised that they would get something for him and hide it in the bushes. Later that day he returned and went straight to the clump of bushes. There was food, as the children had promised: rice and a duck egg. It looked like manna to the hungry boy. He snatched it up and began to eat greedily. A Japanese guard saw him, ran over and knocked the food out of the boy's hands.

"So you want something in belly," he screamed. "I will give it." And he thrust his bayonet again and again into the boy's entrails.

There were accidents, of course. They could not be helped, but they were pretty grim.

One day a bullcart on the way into the prison camp was searched, and a bag of notes was found. Mr. Fred Threatt, the driver, was beaten till unconscious; then Chaplain Alfred C. Oliver, Lieutenant Colonel Edward Mack, Captain Frank Tiffany (Chaplain), Captain Jack Le Mire, with several others, were moved to the municipal jail across the road from the prison camp and in sight of Major H. N. Archer (Pappy) and a group of men, were tied to split bamboo and beaten and tortured for forty-seven days. Colonel Oliver was beaten over the head with the butt of a rifle and his neck was broken. He still wears it strapped in a leather collar. But not one of them talked, not one of them revealed the identity of the people concealed behind the code names, or told how the notes had been smuggled to them.

While this was happening in Cabanatuan with the men, some of the Miss U group were taken to Fort Santiago. Among them were Salome Holland, Julia Bootes (Mrs. Garland L. Hall), Rosalina Escudero, Remedios Ferrer, and they were beaten and tortured and grilled about guerrilla activities and what they knew about smuggling into the POW camp. November 3, 1944, while the Americans were bombing, these girls were sent home all sick, and with terrible sores on their bodies.

But an incident like that did not add to our sense of security. The slightest slip brought such danger and such agony. Just how much danger and agony it could bring was made clear to me when I received a letter from Lieutenant Colonel Elvin C. Barr, giving me a belated description of the brutal execution of some American officers.

In September, 1942, he wrote, Lieutenant Colonel Breitung, Lieutenant Colonel Briggs and Lieutenant Gilbert, U. S. N., had tried to escape from prison. For three days they hid, moving only by night, trying — as all escaped prisoners tried — to reach the hills where the guerrillas would take them in. But they failed.

The rest of the men in the camp saw them being dragged back. One of them was unconscious, his body bumping limply over the ground. Their heads were swollen, their eyes closed. One man had an eye torn out.

Then, in the sight of their comrades, the half-dead men were tied to a post and whipped for three days. When they were cut loose, two of them were still alive, their heads rolling from side to side in agony. At the point of bayonets other American prisoners were forced to dig a shallow hole for a grave. The crowning horror was the burial. The Americans had to put the three men in a hole and then fill it in. They saw the hands of the two who were still alive clawing feebly at the dirt that fell upon them.

Even that was not enough punishment. After the burial, the Japanese seized thirteen officers of the same rank and confined them in a room twelve feet square. There was only one window and that was sealed. There were no sanitary facilities. Just buckets. For fifteen days, the thirteen men did not leave the room. Twice a day they were sent in a few bites of foul smelling lugao (over-cooked soft-boiled rice). At the end of the period, those who were still alive all had beriberi.

These things came closer and closer home. Sooner or later I knew the Japanese would get me. They were bound to.

The Net Closes

I don't know when I first became aware that I was being spied on. A Spanish mestiza, a well-known collaborationist who was living with a Japanese officer, seemed to be trailing me at intervals, and looking at me as though trying to recall a face from her past life. Before the war I had met her casually, but she did not remember my name and she was not positive that I was an American.

A Filipina woman who lived next door to the Spanish mestiza was keeping a close watch on her. Her husband, an American Negro, was a prisoner in Cabanatuan and she had no love for her collaborator neighbor. Because she watched so patiently, she was able, later, to give me a lot of information about that mestiza that was of great help. The mestiza, she said, had got hold of my maid, Maria, and questioned her about me. She wanted to know whether I was an American. Maria told her that she did not know. She had come to me only after the war started and she knew nothing about my past.

"If you stay out of jail until the Japs give the Philippines independence," Ernest Johnson told me one day at the hospital, "I don't think they'll get you." But the net was closing about me and well I knew it. For one thing, there were the guerrillas who were picked up after they left my apartment.

During the months my group had been smuggling supplies into the prison camps, it was inevitable that I should make contact with the guerrilla forces. From their hideouts in the hills, they continually sent men down to Manila for news, food, guns, and to spy out the enemy's plans. If any man was lucky enough to escape the hell of the prison camps, it was the hills that drew him.

The guerrillas were hunted men, subsisting on what they could get secretly. They harassed the Japanese at every turn but they had to keep hidden. No man was too young, none was too old to be of their number. There was only one criterion — trustworthiness. Whole families were members of the various guerrilla bands, the children acting as lookouts, the women nursing, cooking, running messages.

From men in the camps who escaped and from guerrillas who had seen me at the Filipino releases at Camp O'Donnell, the story of the Miss U organization reached the hills. As early as September 1942, my apartment became a meeting place for these men. This was soon after the real work began at Camp O'Donnell. Some Filipinos from Major Edwin P. Ramsey's outfit in the hills found out through a doctor at the camp that I was helping the men there.

One night four guerrillas met at my apartment, bringing a note from Major Ramsey. The guerrilla officers were Captain Emilio M. Asistores, Captain Inigo, Colonel Santos, and Bert Richey. They bore with them written commissions in the guerrilla army for two young men who were to meet them there.

The boys, George Amevic and Bobby Jones, nephew of Papaya, had been given the password and they came in without incident. They knew what they were undertaking and the men who commissioned them knew. They were given money enough to get them to the hills, and issued their guns. As they took the written commissions which made them first lieutenants in the guerrilla forces, they were pretty solemn boys. Those commissions would cost them their lives if the Japanese found them. But the boys wanted to go on fighting. It was infinitely better than capture and internment. At least, they would pay off some scores if they fought.

After the meeting they all left. Next morning I heard that Captain Inigo had been picked up on the Escolta, the main business street of Manila. This was disquieting news. The fate of everyone at the meeting, of my whole group of workers, and of hundreds in the hills might well be in Inigo's hands. I waited anxiously for some word as to what had happened to him, but it was weeks before I learned that he had been set free. He had been tortured but he had not talked.

About a month after the two boys had received their commission in the guerrilla forces at my apartment, I came home about half-past six in the morning. I was very tired. I don't believe I have said that all this time I was continuing to do private nursing at the hospital. To keep my status as a nurse unquestioned, I had to take cases. Anyhow, there was so much sickness and so few who were trained to do anything about it!

That was one of the days when the truck had to be loaded at the convent and sent to the boxcar. I had been busy half the night, but everything had gone well. We did our loading behind the high stone wall back of the Malate Church, and there was little risk of trouble there. The problem, of course, was that you never knew just where trouble was going to arise.

I was making a cup of coffee when I heard a noise on the stairs. Because my mind was occupied with the loading we had been doing, my first thought was that someone had trailed me from the church. As I started toward the door, I began automatically to make up a story that would fit the case. By that time I could concoct a plausible story at the drop of a hat.

I opened the door and there on the stairs was George Amevic, one of the young guerrillas. He was unshaven, filthy, sick and stumbling. He stared at me out of glazed eyes. I pulled him into the apartment and got the story from him.

He had got into the hills, he said, and joined the guerrillas. The Japanese had discovered their camp. There had been a hard fight, several Japanese were killed and two of the guerrillas had bullet wounds. A Japanese had run at George with fixed bayonet and broken his arm above the wrist. But the Japanese were driven off. George tried to get somewhere to have the bone set. As he looked back, he saw the camp in flames. That was the usual procedure, he said. The enemy left nothing. Like locusts, they devoured and destroyed.

For a night and a day, alternately hiding, nursing his arm, and trying to make his way to some village, George finally reached a native house where he was hidden until it was safe to take him to the school at Novaliches. The priests there were taking care of children who had been orphaned by the war. Although they knew the danger of sheltering a guerrilla, they took George in and kept him until his arm became infected. With no means of combating the infection, they advised him to try to get to Manila. They asked whether he knew a doctor there. He said no, but he knew a nurse who would help him if he could reach her.

"Who is she? Are you sure she is to be trusted?"

"I don't know her name. They call her Miss U."

"That's all right," the priest said in relief. "We have heard of her from men passing through. Go to her."

The priest found a guide who knew the country and he took George as far as the outskirts of Manila, where a native was found with a carve tela, and he came to my apartment.

It did not take much of an examination to tell me that this was no case for a nurse. The arm was in bad condition and the boy was flushed and almost incoherent from fever. As soon as I could find a safe messenger, I sent for Dr. Moreta, a Spanish physician whom I could trust, as he had for some time been contributing money for a Major Berry in the prison, and he had put himself at my disposal for cases like this. His daughter was a member of my organization.

The moment he received my message. Dr. Moreta came and said that the arm would have to be broken again and that there was a bad infection. The problem was how to get George to Dr. Moreta's office, as it was out of the question to take him to a hospital.

This was a case where a white woman would be too conspicuous, so I sent for Papaya, who got a carretela and took George to Dr. Moreta's office. She stayed with George during the painful process of rebreaking and setting the arm and dressing the wound which the bayonet had made in the flesh. He could not stay too long at the doctor's office, so after a brief rest he said he was sure he could make the trip back to my apartment. He tried to thank Dr. Moreta, but the Spaniard waved aside his thanks.

"Get well and go on back," he said. "We need every one of you."

When Papaya brought George back, I gave him some food and put him to bed. That night Lee made one of his visits of inspection and I heard a little grunt when he saw the boy in bed in the other room. He came to the door and I lay waiting for his usual sermon and wondering what I could scold him about in return.

"Miss Peggy, who that boy?" he demanded.

I told him and he shook his head. "Very danger."

"He'll have to stay here for a while until his arm gets well," I said. "You needn't come back if you are afraid."

Lee was offended. "Miss Peggy," he said sharply, "you here. I come back to help."

He did too, and he kept watch to make sure that no one found George in the apartment.

As soon as he was able to get around by himself, we tried to help George get back to the hills. He could not go alone, for no one was allowed to approach a guerrilla camp unless he was properly escorted, so we had to keep him in the city until we arranged for a guide. I gave him money and provisions and he left the apartment with his arm in a sling and a leather strap on his wrist. He was to wait with some other Filipino boys who were joining the guerrillas and a guide was on the way to take them to camp.

Poor George set out to meet the other Filipino boys and on the way he encountered a boy whom he had known from childhood. We had carefully arranged a story to account for his broken arm. He was to tell anyone who asked that he had fallen off a bicycle. But this boy was an old friend and George was young and he could not resist boasting.

"I am a member of the guerrillas," he told his friend proudly. "I was in a fight in the hills and a Japanese bayonet did this to me. I am waiting to go back now."

His friend raised his arm above his head and held it there for a moment and some Japanese came running out of a doorway across the street and captured him. It was as easy as that. He was brutally beaten in Fort Santiago. Someone who saw him after his release said he was reeling like a punch-drunk fighter; his teeth had been knocked out. But he had not talked. Otherwise, I would have been picked up.

Not long after that, I sent messages to the guerrilla camp that there were three more boys waiting to join them. One evening a Filipina girl came in to see me crying. "Miss U," she sobbed, 'Freddie, he is tite. He is tite, poor Freddie."

I was exasperated, thinking she meant the boy was drunk, and that was a criminal act of carelessness on his part. I told her what I'd say to him when I saw him.

"No," the girl cried out, "not drunk! Tite." I realized then she meant he was dead.

Those three boys seemed to be marked out for bad luck. I sent for the other two, George and Frank, to warn them to be careful. Frank told me his story. He had worked at Cavite Naval Base and his wife had been killed in the early bombing of Manila. He had walked from the suburb where they had lived with his little six-year-old daughter, knowing she would be cared for at Holy Ghost convent. He was carrying her picture in his pocket.

"Find out how she is," he begged me. "See whether she needs anything."

But I dared not go to the convent and inquire about Americans. Anyhow, the nuns were driven out before long. I suppose Frank's little girl was with them, but where she went I have no idea. I kept thinking of her grandparents in the States, waiting and wondering what had become of her. But I could not have held on to my own sanity if I had let myself dwell too much on these things.

When the two boys left my apartment, they separated, one walking on one side of the street, the other crossing over. The Japanese came swarming up, seized Frank, knocked him down, and began to beat him savagely. There was nothing George could do to help and he ran away, but they caught him too. It was some time before I saw him again.

I had got a jar of brown sugar that weighed about twenty-five pounds and I was sitting on a curb, hoping a boy with a pushcart would come along and carry it for me. Down the middle of the road came a pitiful figure, a man dragging his feet, wearing only a pair of ragged, dirty pants. His stringy hair hung about his face. He was mumbling. At first I thought he was an escaped slave laborer from Nichols Field and wondered what I could do about him. Then I recognized him. It was George.

I called to him but he paid no attention. I ran out into the street. "Don't you know me, George?"

The vacant eyes just stared. Finally he said, "Yes, you helped us." Then he lapsed into mumbling again.

There was a hospital for the indigent nearby and I took him there. "I'm hungry," he said clearly once, and then mumbled again.

At the hospital I said that I knew the boy and he was ill. The attendant did not ask questions. She could guess.

I got the sugar delivered at last and went to the hospital the next morning. George was gone. The attendants said they had fed him, bathed him, given him clean clothes. The last anyone saw of him he was walking out, muttering, "I've got to find him. I've got to find him."

For days I was haunted by the thought of that poor insane boy wandering around until he died. I think he was worrying about Frank; perhaps he felt guilty because he had run away when Frank was beaten.

The fate of those boys drove home the cold certainty that there was danger all around us. It came even closer when Father Lalor telephoned late one evening to say that he thought the Japanese were after me and I had better not stay in the apartment that night. I hastily gathered together my pajamas and toothbrush in a little bundle and Sassie Susie, Scatterbrain and I cleared out of the place. We waited in the shadow of some hibiscus bushes for a bicycle with a seat for the passenger in front — the substitute for a taxi in wartime Manila. When it came I climbed on, but I had not gone far before I saw that the Japanese were stopping and searching every sort of vehicle that passed.

One of them stopped my bicycle and walked around it. Then he reached out and snatched the bundle from my hands. It was long, thin package and looked like a gun. He bent it in the middle and when he found it was soft, he threw it back. Then he took the driver's coco-cloth cape and shook it until its dry, straw-like fibers rattled, and threw it down on the ground. He was getting madder by the minute. He asked who I was and I said a Kangafu. At length he let me go. I stayed three nights and days at the home of Papaya; then I went back to the apartment. After all, there was no other place to go.

The riskiest part of my work was collecting guns and ammunition for the guerrillas. It was not long after Father Lalor's warning that a boy who had been able to get some guns for me came up to say that there was a guerrilla in town who wanted to help. At that time I did not need a new contact and I never wanted to take on anyone who was not absolutely necessary. I was hesitant to let the man come up but as it was about time for a runner to come down from the hills, I took a chance. Perhaps this was the man.

The moment he entered the room I was cold with suspicion. This was a mistake. I knew it. The man stayed for about an hour, telling me of his work. He showed me a lot of propaganda pictures and a new magazine that he claimed was published in the United States, offering it as proof that he was in contact with the States. Before he left he told me that he would be glad to supply as much money as I needed. I looked at him blankly and said that I needed money for nothing.

Sassie Susie was in the apartment when the man called and as soon as he left she whirled around to me. "That man is not a guerrilla," she said. "I know it. I feel sure of it."

There on the chair where he had been sitting was a revolver. We hunted carefully and found two bullets hidden under the typewriter. It was a plant, of course. That meant the Japanese were going to search the place. We got rid of that revolver and the ammunition so fast it made our heads swim.

At least the Japanese did not keep us in suspense. About midnight the telephone rang. When I answered a woman's voice said, "Hello," and then there was a click as the receiver hung up.

Ten to one that meant trouble coming, but I had had a hard day and I went to bed to sleep. I was awakened by a shuffling on the stairs and a heavy banging on the iron grilled door that brought my heart into my throat. Maria came in, looking petrified.

"The Japs are here, ma'am," she said.

I suppose I was as ready for them then as I ever would be. I swung my feet out of bed and reached for my housecoat. "Well," I replied, "let them in."

It seemed to me there were at least fifty soldiers in the party. There were so many they could not all crowd into the apartment. The first one in the room went straight to the typewriter table.

"Use this much?" he asked.

"I'm just learning to type," I said and showed him the book of instructions.

He lifted the typewriter and looked decidedly surprised. There was no doubt in my mind then that the bullets had been planted.

"Where are your guns?" he asked.

"I have no guns," I replied.

With typical Japanese dexterity and patience, those soldiers literally took the place apart. They shook out every piece of linen in the drawers, searched every match box, powder box, pillow, picture frame, and book. They even opened two bottles of perfume.

Meanwhile, the man in charge of the search party was questioning me: name, profession, passport. For eight hours he kept it up tirelessly, hammering away particularly about my constant trips to the areas of the prison camps.

I adopted the role of a tired, waspish old maid nurse and stuck to it. I showed him my permit and explained what I was trying to do for the "needy of Cabanatuan." I explained my Lithuanian citizenship.

At seven in the morning he was still at it: "Why do you have so many books? .... Where is your gun? .... Why do you go to the provinces?"

At seven-thirty the man in charge telephoned for instructions, forbade me to leave the city or move my quarters, called his men together and off they went.

I was so tired and dazed from the long relentless questioning without sleep that I could hardly move. But I had to report to the hospital. There were two emergency cases there whom I was nursing; both of them, as it happened, were women who were members of my group. It looked as though I had come to the end of my rope, but there was nothing to do but hang on. I set out for the hospital.

Caught!

It was on the morning of Friday, September 28, that I set out for the hospital. Maria was going to Mass later in the morning, so the apartment would be empty. As I left the house I knew that I was being watched. The hospital too was under surveillance. It is unpleasant to walk deliberately into a trap.

It was about eleven o'clock in the morning, and I was looking after one of my patients, a woman named Zenia Jastin, who was ill with cancer, when it happened. The tramp of heavy feet in the corridor coming toward the ward where I was. I stiffened up. They were at the door, eight of them, fully armed, bayonets fixed.

"You will come," one of them said, and I went. The eight Japanese fell into formation around me and we marched down the hall and out of the building. I was grateful now for the dark glasses which I had taken to wearing ever since I had become a Lithuanian. If I was going to make a practice of telling lies, I wanted something to hide my eyes, which are always a dead give-away when one is frightened. I had been wearing the things for months and right now they gave me a curious sense of protection.

I didn't know where they were taking me but it was probably Fort Santiago. That was where people usually went to be questioned. They always came out looking the worse for wear. Fort Santiago was not far away and I found myself wishing it were much, much farther. Perhaps I was looking my last upon Manila, upon the sun-drenched street, upon the sun itself. Life can seem very sweet when you think you may be at the end of it. I could hear myself whispering, "Just a little longer, just a little longer." I stopped that in a hurry and began checking over my story in my mind, making sure that it was all clear, that I had not overlooked anything.

It was Fort Santiago, all right. That old fort had had a number of flags over it in its time — five, I think. It was on the Pasig River and it had once had a moat around it. Santiago was a citadel of the ancient Spanish walled city of Manila, a place of colossal masonry walls and slimy dungeons. The dungeons were still there, just as foul and damp as they had been in the past. Pre-war tourists found Santiago delightfully picturesque. I didn't, but then I saw it under something less than ideal conditions.

The Japanese soldiers took me into a large sunny room on the second floor. Through its open, screened side, I could see the lovely patio, the soft lawn, the flowers. Across it lowered the prison itself with its stone cells, many of them out over the water. In the days of the Spaniards, the floors had had openings through which the bodies of luckless captives could be dropped into the river with scarcely a sound.

Perhaps, after all, war has not changed so much — or people. We read history as though past things were dead things, with no relation to ourselves. And when the same things happen again, we are terribly surprised. Someday, tourists may visit the ruins of places I know where men were starved and tortured and executed. And all that pain and agony will have no meaning for them. They'll pay an admission fee because the place is quaint, or because it is a historical shrine. But it won't teach them anything.

Seated at a table was a Japanese officer, his saber at his side. Across the table was a younger Japanese, who was the interpreter. Near the entrance a Filipino lay on a cot, his face covered. All during the ordeal of that first day, he lay like a dead man, like one of the figures in an ancient tapestry, which kept before the neophyte the constant and awful reminder of death. Who he was I never knew, nor why he was there. The hallway outside was full of spectators, but I was only dimly aware of them.

The interpreter told me to sit down at the end of the table. I did as I was told. Then he ordered me to put my hands on the table, palms down, arms straight out. It was a strained, uncomfortable position that made me feel very helpless. My heart was pounding thickly at the base of my throat, and I swallowed. I wanted my voice to be steady. Whatever happened, I swore to myself, I would never give them any satisfaction by showing fear or by screaming. The first part of the vow I kept; there were a few times, later on, when I broke the second part. You can stand only so much pain.

The interpreter sat to my left. The officer with the saber sat across from me. Before them was a stack of large square papers. It didn't seem possible that anyone could have collected that much information about me.

"You will swear before your God," the interpreter said, "to tell the truth."

My mouth felt like cotton. "Yes, I will swear," I said.

"The Japanese very smart people," he said. "They cannot be fooled. You better not lie. We can tell."

"I wouldn't dream of trying to fool you," I protested. "Why should I?"

"We know American and Englishmen are easy on women," he went on. "Japanese are not. If you lie to us, you will be tortured just like a man."

I had no reason to think he was bluffing.

Then, to my surprise, the two men got up and left the room. After a while a Japanese boy came in with food: rice and fish about six inches long, officers' rations. I thought of the condemned man who ate a hearty breakfast but I could not swallow. I did change my position though and rubbed my arms to get the circulation back in them.

The two men returned, the officer's saber rattling as he sat down. My skin tightened. It was going to begin now.

"You did not eat chow," the interpreter said.

"No. I ate just before I came. I'm not hungry."

Then the questions began. Where was I born? When? I was Rosena Utinsky, a Lithuanian citizen, born in Kovno. I had the proper papers, thanks to Elizabeth Kummer, which I showed them.

Where was my apartment key? I gave it to them. Where was my maid? So they had been to the apartment that morning and found it empty. I knew darned well there was nothing incriminating for them to find there. Yet they set importance on queer things. When the huge search party had gone through my apartment they had taken away some menu cards from night clubs and famous restaurants which I had visited on my trip to the States in 1940. There had not seemed to be much point in it and I had been amused to think they took the menu cards and overlooked three thousand pesos I had hidden, ready to smuggle to Cabanatuan.

Did my maid go to church every day? What time did she come home at night? Between questions the two men talked rapidly to each other in Japanese. There seemed to be some sharp differences of opinion between them, and from behind the dark glasses I watched, trying to get some clue to the questions that were coming, some hint as to their thoughts from the sound of words which had no meaning for me. I sat with my arms stretched out. The muscles in the upper arms and at the base of my neck were beginning to jump with fatigue.

Here it comes. When was I in the United States? In 1940. Why? For a vacation. On what boat did I go? This was a tricky one. I could not tell the truth because I had gone on the *Grant*, which was an Army transport. The *President Hayes*, I told them, and prayed fervently that there were no records of the *Grant*'s passenger list. What was in that stack of papers they kept shuffling?

Better not let my attention wander. You can't slip up on the details. It's the details that catch you every time. It's the little things you have to watch.

What day did I reach America? Did they have a record of sailing and arrival dates in that stack of papers? If they did, I was sunk. I'd better tell the truth whenever I could. There had to be some guideposts of truth to cling to. Well, here goes.

"I arrived on June twenty-second."

Where? San Francisco. Why? I wanted to see the exposition. Then where? Treasure Island. Why? To see it. Then where? One thing I know they have in that stack of papers. The menu cards. They are trying to check my itinerary from them.

Before I could reorganize that trip in my mind they changed tack. Why do you wear dark glasses? Do you need them? Yes, I had to have them. I had a lot of trouble with my eyes and the light bothered them. Then why did I have plain glasses too? Certainly I didn't need both pairs. I figured that I would not be doing much reading at Fort Santiago, but I'd be doing a lot of talking. I'd hang on to the dark glasses. So they took the other pair. Then they took my shoes and the bobby pins from my hair. I was wearing a tiny gold cross hung around my neck by a fine little chain. When they reached for it, I drew back.

"Must you take that?" I asked. "I've never had it off."

The interpreter snatched at it, ripping it from my neck. "Might swallow and die," he explained.

They switched back to my visit to the States. Then where you go? To San Antonio. When you get there? The Fourth of July.

That did it! The officer jumped from his chair, purple with rage, the veins in his forehead distended, and struck me full in the face with his fist. The blow knocked me out of the chair. I think it must have been then, that very first day, that they broke my jaw.

I fell sidewise, a bit behind the chair, and lay there in abject terror, seeing the officer's hand close on the hilt of the saber. I had seen enough beheadings to know what these men were capable of doing. I didn't dare move.

The interpreter stood waiting. Finally the officer said, "Kura! Kura!" an almost untranslatable word that means everything from "all right" to "let's get going." Painfully I pulled myself up and for good measure the officer kicked me as I rose. My mouth was full of blood and broken teeth. I spat them out on the floor.

I hope I never hear anything again about the stoical Oriental. At the slightest excitement, the Japanese begin to scream. Already the room that had been so quiet was a seething commotion. The officer was screaming at me. The spectators in the hallway were jabbering. Only the Filipino lay on the cot, unmoving.

"Why you say Fourth July?" the officer yelled. "Big American feast day." So he did know English, after all.

I sat down again, my arms stretched out in front of me. I was shaking and could not control it. "You told me to speak the truth," I said as quietly as I could manage. "I am. That was the day I arrived in San Antonio. I don't know about the feast day. I just decided to go there and that's the day I arrived."

Why you go there? I couldn't mention relatives. Like a flash I remembered some big advertising posters. There was a rodeo there, I said quickly. I had never seen a rodeo. What is a rodeo? I tried to explain, pantomiming the movements of a rider on a bronco. Then one of the bystanders said brightly, "yes, yes, rodeo. I know. Cow fight."

I embroidered on my description of a rodeo as long as I could. It was gaining me a little time until I could steady my nerves again and be ready for more questions. My cheek ached from the blow and it was beginning to swell. The pain kept distracting my attention from the questions.

Where did I go next? Chicago. Why? Well, my aunt in Canada went there once and told me so much about the lake and the buildings and the drive that I wanted to see them too. Why hadn't I gone to Canada instead? I grew up there, didn't I? Then why did I go to the United States? Because there was so little time. I already knew Canada. I wanted to see new places with what money I had.

Where did I stay in Chicago? The Y.W.C.A. It was cheaper and would give me more money for sightseeing.

Then where? New York. I seemed to be spending a lot of money for a nurse on vacation so I stressed my economies. I had taken a bus to the fair because it was cheaper than a cab. My jaw was throbbing like mad. It didn't seem possible one blow could hurt in so many different ways, mouth and gums and teeth, all with separate aches.

"You went to America on an American passport," the interpreter said.

What the deuce could be in that stack of papers anyhow? "Oh, no," I said. "I traveled on an immigration card." Someone had once described the process to me and I passed it on to the Japanese. I told them glibly about the yellow card I was given. I told them how we foreign passengers were lined up, Russians, French, and I was the only Lithuanian. We signed our names in a book, I said, and then we were given a card and told we could stay for six months, but we must report to the Immigration Office every so often.

They went back to Canada again. Why hadn't I gone there? I remembered how Naomi had been slapped for answering the same question in different words, so I was careful to repeat myself when I explained again about my aunt's visits to Chicago. And I explained it again. And again. "You go to New York to see Fair? You are American?" There were a lot of Japanese looking at the Fair, I told them, and they certainly weren't Americans. This was the first flash of spirit I had shown and every second I expected that fist to crunch into my face again, or the officer's fingers to tighten over his saber. I was almost dead from the strain of holding out my arms, from my sore mouth and jaw. At least, that is what I thought then. Later on I learned what real pain is like.

Now they were asking why I came back to the Philippines. Up to now, whenever I had found an answer I was sure of, an answer that I knew could not be contradicted by anything they might have in those papers — what in hell was in those papers? — I had expanded on it, to give me a breathing space. Then I saw that they were encouraging me to talk on. I'd better watch out. You don't get into trouble for talking too little. You get into trouble for talking too much.

Why you leave America when you have such a good time? As a Lithuanian, I pointed out, I was practically a German. War was coming. The Americans would put me in an internment camp. Anyhow, I knew no one in America. My friends were here. My work was here. What boat you come back on? It was a Maru boat, I said. That was logical enough. Every Japanese boat of any size was a Maru boat. A sick woman advertised she was traveling to the Orient and wanted a nurse for the voyage. I applied for the job so my passage would be paid. They took me because I did not expect to return to the States and they would have to pay my passage only one way.

Where was she going? Hongkong. Whoops, that did it! I saw the Japanese exchange a glance and remembered that Maru boats went only to

Honolulu at that time. We changed at Honolulu, of course, I explained hastily, for a boat to take us on to Hongkong. What boat? The *Saurholt*. They didn't say anything. The old lady died in Hongkong, I went on, and I had come back to Manila.

Better be careful here. This is where the story is thin. There were no records of my arrival in Manila. I had to account for that in some way. Then I remembered hearing that the British boat *Anhue* had put in at Manila on December 8, 1941, and then had sailed without warning. The British consul had got word of the bombing of Pearl Harbor and ordered the boat out so fast that it left behind no record of its passengers, many of whom, indeed, had been stranded by that unscheduled sailing.

I described how I had tried to get hold of my papers but that I had not worried about it because it never occurred to me that anyone would want any record of my being on the boat.

They veered around again. Tell about my father. He died when I was a little girl. What was my mother's name? I invented one. I was Lithuanian, wasn't I? Then why didn't I speak Lithuanian? Once more I repeated the story of my childhood which had come to seem almost as real to me as the one I had actually lived. My aunt had taken me to live with her in Canada when I was very small. We always spoke English because my aunt was English.

"We know you American. We put you in Santo Tomas."

"Fine," I retorted. "Then I won't have to earn my living any more."

The two Japanese leaned back and lighted cigarettes and I tried to relax a little. The sunlight was not so bright now. There were shadows stretching toward the east. It had been a very long day.

The interpreter began to stack the papers neatly together. Were they through with me? The officer rose, then the interpreter. I dared not move.

"Get up! We go now." They beckoned to a guard. I got up stiffly. My arms tingled as I let them drop to my side. My jaw throbbed. There was dried blood on my mouth. My gums, where the teeth had been broken, were sore and swollen. My bare feet made almost no sound as I went through the doorway with the guard. The Filipino still lay motionless on his cot.

We went along a hall, down the stairs, across the patio, through the arches, and down a narrow corridor. They pushed me into a cell and the door clanged shut.

Torture

As SOON as I heard the guard go away, I jerked off my dark glasses and looked around. I was in a cell about eight feet long and five feet wide. The only light came from an aperture above the door. At one end of the cell there was a bucket of drinking water, but no water in which to wash. At the other end there was a hole in which a covered bucket was lowered, the only sanitary facility provided. Every morning the bucket was taken from behind the wall, emptied and returned to the hole.

The cells were built between two walls. In the inside wall were the doors leading out into the corridor. Beyond the outer wall was the outside wall of the prison. Between the two, there was a narrow passageway for the prisoners who performed the menial tasks of the cell block. These were priests who, because the people seemed to hold them in veneration, had the greatest humiliations heaped upon them by the Japanese. They were forced to strip down to a G-string and empty the slops of the other prisoners.

That night there were seven women in the cell. Only two of them could speak English but they all crowded around me, whispering, avid for news. It was like a thirst upon them. None of them had had any word of what was happening in the world outside the walls in over three months.

"When will the Americans come?" they asked. "When will the Americans come?"

I told them all I could of what was going on, sketched the news that had come by shortwave radio. And those who could speak English retailed the news to the others and told me about my cellmates. I was the only one, it turned out, who had not been committed to prison by the Japanese courts for one offense or another.

One of the two women who could speak English was the wife of Dr. Vicente Domingo. On August 26, 1943, the doctor had been taken from his home to his office by a detachment of Japanese. There he had been commanded to open his safe in which he kept thousands of pesos. He gave his captors the combination but they could not manage it and they forced him to open the safe. Then, in their greed to snatch the contents as fast as they could, they allowed him to sit at his desk while they looted.

That was a mistake, for Dr. Domingo kept a revolver in his desk drawer. He whipped it out and shot all four men. Three of them died, but the fourth was only wounded. The doctor grabbed his valuables and fled. The Japanese whom he had failed to kill notified the police and soldiers went to his home. Mrs. Domingo was pregnant but that did not prevent them from beating her unmercifully, as well as the doctor's young brother. Then the two of them were dragged off to Fort Santiago to be held as hostages. The three small Domingo children were left with servants. Mrs. Domingo was not questioned, but she lay in the cell week after week, her one hope being that her baby need not be born in that terrible place.

Another of my cellmates was a Filipina woman whose crime was having more rice in her house than the Japs allowed. Still another had been arrested for profiteering. She had sold some rice for a few cents more than the price set. She was fined eighty pesos and given ninety days in jail. Now she was working out her fine, but she had no idea how long she would be jailed since her "wages" were what her captors wanted them to be. She could only hope that deliverance would come soon, though nothing in her daily routine could give her any assurance that it would.

And over and over, while we exchanged those hurried, furtive confidences, the women repeated, "When will the Americans come?" That they would come, they never doubted. But when? How long would they be called upon to endure this horror? I could not give them a satisfactory answer.

Suddenly the slot beside the door opened and a face peered through. "Kneel!" the guard said sharply. "Why you talk?" Without warning his fist shot through the slot and struck me. That was the way I learned the "no talking" rule.

For supper they gave us lugao, foul-smelling rice boiled in water until it looked and tasted like clothes starch. We had that for breakfast too. That was the only thing I had to eat for the thirty-two days I spent in Fort Santiago.

I crumpled down on the floor with weariness. There was no place to sit. We slept at night on the stone floor without even a newspaper to cover us. My jaw ached like mad, I was thirsty and my body was clammy.

That night I lay down on the damp cold floor of the cell and tried to sleep. I would need all the strength I had and it was important to keep a clear head. But I kept going over and over my story, testing it, trying to find any loopholes. I could not plan ahead. There was no use guessing what they would ask next. One thing sure — I had beaten them for one day at least. I had made my story stick that far. I went to sleep at last.

The next morning I learned the prison routine which never varied. It was as rigid as that of a military barracks. At seven there was roll call, which we must answer. A woman who knew Japanese taught us to answer roll call in Japanese, which was required of us. How many prisoners there were in Fort Santiago I never learned, but there were more than three hundred at that one end of the cell block. I would keep count as the roll call started every morning, so I knew that there were that many within earshot of my cell.

Every hour the sentries changed outside our door and we had to stand as the sentry walked by, and bow during the morning worship.

A night on the cell floor had not improved the appearance of my white uniform. My hair was uncombed and they had taken my hairpins. I had not washed for twenty-four hours. My bare feet still had the grime of the corridors on them. I wiped the blood off my mouth but my jaw was still swollen and hurt horribly. All my teeth on the left side felt too big for their sockets.

I began to see now why the other women in my cell were in such a horrible condition. Some of them had not washed or changed their clothes in at least three months. No care of any sort was permitted them. They had menstruated at first with no protection. After a while that stopped; they were all so undernourished that it could not go on.

The Japanese came for me that second day and it was a surprise, as we went across the patio, to see the sun shining as brightly as it had shone the day before. It would be easy, after a few weeks in a dark cell, to forget what it is like to see the sun, and to hear normal homely sounds. It made me feel almost good to see the daylight. What worried me most that morning was not the questioning. It was that they would hit me again. If they did, please let it be on the other side. And not because I felt like turning the other cheek, either. If they hit that left jaw again, I felt certain I'd just plain die right there.

This time I paid more attention to where we were going. We passed a lot of little rooms like offices, with people standing around, just as they had done the day before. Some Japanese officers were standing near the door of the room where I had already been questioned. The same officer and interpreter were waiting for me.

It began just as the first day had done. The interpreter asked questions; the officer sat there and pretended not to know English.

Well, it went on, over and over. Where was I born? Who were my parents? I stopped thinking about anything but being Rosena Utinsky. It was a sort of anesthetic, not letting myself think of anything else. Rosena Utinsky, answering questions. Over and over.

Without warning the officer slapped me across the face. Luckily it wasn't the left side. He just reached out and hit me, flat-handed. I jerked away.

"Now have you made up your mind to tell the truth?"

"I have been telling the truth all the time."

The officer slapped me again. And again.

And the questions went on. They hoped, if they kept hammering at me, I would slip somewhere in the story. My brain felt as though their words really were little hammers, pounding until it was almost numb. But I didn't dare let it get too numb. Then I would slip and they would have me. It was better to be alive, even in this filthy hole, than dead in a ditch in the yard.

That afternoon they took me back to the cell again. This time I remembered about the talking. I was almost glad when seven o'clock came and I could lie down. At least the aches from the stone floor were in different places. I could rest my arms, which had been stretched out all day on the table. And that night several of the women were taken out of the cell. We were not quite so cramped for space, and there was a little more water to drink. But still no water for washing.

It was the fifth day I remember best because that was the day the torture started. As soon as I got inside the room that morning, I knew I was in for it. The interpreter was looking too happy to suit me. I had learned a long time before that when the Japanese looked happy it was a bad sign for the rest of us. And there, right on top of the pile of papers I saw my Red Cross application for volunteer work, the application which I had signed, in October 1941, as an American! There was only one way they could have gotten it — through the Red Cross itself. And that, I knew in a flash, meant the Filipino doctor who had turned me in to the officials during that second trip to Bataan.

The officer motioned for me to sit down. I was so scared I could hardly move but I sat down, thinking frantically, making up and discarding one story after another. This would have to be good. I had to come through this or I would never leave Fort Santiago.

The interpreter wasted no time. He tossed the paper in front of me. You write that? I still had no story. I leaned over, peering at it, playing for time.

"I can't see very well. Let me take it close to the window."

I held it gripped tightly as I walked slowly to the window, hoping my hands would not shake and rattle the paper. I held it up to the light and read it, word by word. Then I nodded my head. I could see both of them expand with satisfaction.

"Yes, I wrote it," I said, "but it wasn't true. I'm not an American. I told you the truth about where I was born but I lied to the Red Cross. I was afraid they wouldn't let me work for them if they knew I was a foreigner."

The officer made a gesture and the interpreter got up and pushed a bench near the table. He pointed to it.

My heart turned over as I looked at it. But there were no wires attached. That was something. I had heard about the electric machines the Japanese used for torture here, unspeakable torture. There was an electrode shaped like a curling iron which was applied to women. They would be stripped naked and forced to lie on the floor on top of wet sacks. A Japanese would stand on the woman's stomach, the electrode was thrust up the vagina and the current turned on. The agony was beyond any words. The wet sacks made a perfect conductor and the woman flung her legs and arms around madly in her suffering. One of these women was taken out of Fort Santiago in a strait jacket and sent to Santo Tomas. She was in the psychopathic ward there and finally taken to an asylum for the hopelessly insane. Another victim, who had been raped before the torture, was insane for awhile and later seemed to be nearly normal. But during the shelling of Manila, she lapsed back into a raving delirium from which she never recovered.

But this was just a bench. Its only unusual feature was that it had thin split bamboo across it for a seat — and split bamboo is as sharp as knives! I pulled down my skirt and sat down easily, carefully.

"No, no," the interpreter said. "Kneel on it."

My skirt didn't help much, though it did protect my knees a little. I let myself down gingerly on my bare shins, and leaned forward to rest my weight on my arms on the table.

The interpreter pushed them off. "Sit back," he ordered. "Sit back."

So I sat back on my heels, the bamboo cutting into my legs. That day they really went to work on me. The Red Cross application was the first concrete proof they had found that I was an American. They screamed at me. They tried to tangle me up in questions. They went back to my frequent trips to Camp O'Donnell and Cabanatuan. They said over and over that I was an American. And the officer kept slapping me.

It went on for hours, the sharp edges of the bamboo cutting deeper and deeper into my legs. The bone is close to the surface of the shins. The muscles in my hips and thighs cramped and ached. The questions drilled on and on. And the officer walked around and around the bench, looking to see whether I had found a position that would keep my legs from hurting. Because I hadn't, that made him mad too, and he slapped me over and over. But I was in so much pain every other way, with my legs bleeding, my muscles cramped, that a slap more or less hardly counted.

Only now and then, when they would abruptly stop questioning me and lean back for a leisurely smoke, did I try to shift my weight from one leg to the other to ease the pain a little.

At length they said, "Get up."

I tried but I could not move my legs.

They started to shout and scream again. "Get up!"

This time I managed to move but I could not get up. I tumbled over on the floor. Pressure on the blood vessels from holding that one position so long had cut off circulation to my legs and feet. The officer stood yelling. I struggled for a while before I could straighten out. At last I could get up, then I could stand, then I could walk.

My lacerated legs hurt worse now that circulation was restored. The thought of the lugao made me sick. I stumbled back to my cell. Sometime, I thought, I would have to eat more to keep up my strength — but not tonight. All I could do was lie on the floor and try to protect my cut legs from the dirt. That night I was in so much pain I almost forgot that I had beaten them again. They had not found a loophole in my story yet or they would never have let me go.

The next day we didn't go to the sunny room overlooking the patio. Instead, they took me upstairs to a long room with a piano. It must have been a sort of recreation room, but not for me. They had decided to try something else. They tied my hands behind my back, attached a rope to the tied wrists and jerked me up several feet above the floor. While I hung there, they screamed questions at me again and again and beat me with their fists.

That was the beginning of days of alternate tortures. One day would be the bamboo bench, the next day a beating. My legs never healed. And my back was a mess. They got tired of using their fists and began to beat me with the flat side of a bayonet, then with a leather belt that cut across my back.

The legs got worse. It wasn't just the bamboo. When they let me down from the beatings, they would lower me to about two feet from the floor and then drop me. Instinctively my knees would draw up and I would fall on the torn flesh. The first few times I thought the fall would kill me, but I lived through thirty-two days. And sometimes, just for variety, when his cigarette was burning brightly, the officer ground the burning coal into my arm.

All that time, all those days and days, I never screamed. I let them go ahead and do what they liked to me and didn't make a sound. But toward the end, when my shins were a mass of running sores, they took a stick, and scraped the sores. I yelled then.

One day, after I had been hanging by my wrists practically the whole day long — it is simple to say, it is harder to imagine; your arms are tied behind you, they pull you up with your weight on your twisted arms; the questions hammer on and on; without warning, at any minute, the belt comes lashing across your back, you jerk on the end of the rope; well, that's how that day was — the officer who had been torturing me took me back to my cell. I staggered on the staircase, and he said quickly, solicitously, "Be careful. You might hurt yourself."

All the time I was in prison I noticed that our treatment changed with the news. If the Japanese military suffered defeats or setbacks, we paid for it. If President Roosevelt talked to the people, describing what had been accomplished, things went badly for us. Our slim rations of lugao and water were cut. When Hongkong was bombed, we really felt it.

The fear and ugliness did not end at night when I was dragged back to my cell. There was a Japanese captain who seemed to be in command of the wing of the prison where I was held. At night he sat at a little table in the corridor not far from my cell. He was always drinking. He would shout for a Filipino to bring a glass of liquor, not the clear saki which the Japs ordinarily drink, but brown, rather like dark whisky. He would drink it down in a gulp and then throw the glass up against the far wall of the corridor so the pieces would fly into our cell, all over us.

We would pick out the flying splinters of glass. They didn't bother me much. What worried me was that my legs and back were a mass of open sores, my uniform was unbelievably filthy, and I was afraid of infection.

One night when I got back to my cell, weak and sick, one of the Filipina women whispered that one of the watchers that day had been the dread Yamashita, the Tiger himself. I didn't care. I had reached the point where all I could think of at night was, "One more day and I've stuck to my story. If only I can do it again tomorrow." I couldn't think ahead more than one day.

The days are blurred — the bamboo bench, the beatings — but some things stand out. There was the day when I was being led to torture and I heard a Filipino boy whistling "The Stars and Stripes Forever." It sounded like angels singing. The Jap guard asked what it was.

"A Filipino love song," the boy replied, and he chuckled.

There was the day when the Jap officer shouted at me that he knew I was a liar. He had found my name as a passenger on a boat and I was listed as an American! I had never been on the boat in my life, and all I thought at the time was that the Japanese were almost as good liars as I was. It was not until I was on my way back to the cell that evening that the full importance of the accusation soaked into my tired brain. They were bluffing. They had no evidence. They could not prove anything. They believed me — they believed that I was Rosena Utinsky.

When that idea finally dawned on me, tears ran down my dirty face. A little light was breaking.

Solitary

They came to the conclusion, I think, that they could not break me through pain. But there was one thing left. They might be able to break me through my spirit. So while the days were filled with torture, the nights became an unspeakable nightmare. Night after night, I looked through the bars and saw the incredible things that man can do to man. I saw beatings and torture. I saw living men brought in and their dead bodies dragged out. One night I saw five Filipinos, four men and a woman, beheaded in that narrow corridor.

I watched because I had to watch, and the Japs hoped that if my own pain would not make me break, the agony of others might do the trick. That can be the only reason for the hideous thing that followed — the very peak of horror.

That night the drunken captain came to his table in the corridor as usual. About nine o'clock there was the sound of movement, and then through the bars I could see the man as he was brought nearer. He was an American, I was sure of that. His feet were hobbled and he could take steps only about six inches long. His hands were handcuffed behind him. At every step of his slow walk the Japanese were beating and kicking him. They brought him up to my cell and he leaned against the bars.

He had been bayoneted or shot in the shoulder. I could see the wound, see the blood running down from his shoulder, dripping down his arm and onto his hand, which was covered with caked blood. His clothes were streaked with it.

The captain ordered him thrown into the cell next to mine. I couldn't sleep. I lay there thinking of the poor fellow, longing to cleanse that wound, to try and stop the bleeding. And I was helpless.

About one o'clock in the morning they dragged him out and propped him up against my cell so I could see.

I lay on the floor while the prisoner leaned against the bars. I saw the captain take a belt and wrap the end around his hand. My stomach turned over. I knew what that meant — the beating with the buckle end. And this man was so sick and so hurt. I felt every nerve in my body grow tight and raw as I waited for the lash of the belt. It came, right across the man's face and I could feel it as though it were my own. I knew how that buckle felt. All day it had come lashing across my back. But this was worse.

The man did not cry out — perhaps he would not give them that satisfaction, perhaps he was just too weak. Again and again the buckle struck and I could hear the sighing sound as it cut in. Blood and pieces of flesh flew all over me. Abruptly the beating stopped. The man was pushed and dragged back into the next cell. All night he moaned in a sort of whimper, like a little hurt baby.

The next night the same thing happened. This time the man was much weaker. He just shook his head a little and it would bend against the blows. Again the blood and flesh flew, spattering me. And the wound in his shoulder looked worse, the caked blood still covered him. The same drunken captain wielded the belt, bringing the buckle end down with a crunching sound.

He screamed, "I can kill you if I want to! I will kill you tomorrow!"

Then the man was thrown back into his cell. That night he was so weak I could barely hear him moan.

When I left the next morning for my usual day of questions and torture — I can't remember now whether it was to the bamboo bench or to the hanging and beating — the thought of that poor man made it easier for me to take the worst they could give. They gave it all right, trying to trap me with questions, to break me with pain. But I remembered that my filthy dress was all spattered with what I knew was American blood, shed to make me talk and endanger more Americans.

The third night came. I was sore all over, I could not eat. I lay dreading the moment when that drunken beast would scream for the sick man to be dragged out, and for the buckle to slash across his scarred, bloody, helpless face.

And the time came. The prisoner was dragged out again and propped against my cell. The captain wrapped the belt around his hand. The blows began to fall.

Then I knew that the pitiful thing that had once been a good-looking, clean-cut American was only flesh now. Weakened from loss of blood as he was, terrified of breaking, tortured with pain, the last blow had been too much. I saw him slump, then slide slowly down the bars to the floor. They took him by the neck and dragged him out. I don't know in what unmarked grave they dumped that poor, battered body.

The drunken captain lurched up to the bars of my cell. He stuck his fist through the bars and screamed, "Y, Utinsky! Tomorrow morning I take you to graveyard!"

I sank down on the floor. I was numb. I couldn't sleep. I thought of Jack, who was dead, and of my son Charles, who did not even know where I was. I lay there till the dirty gray light of morning came into the cell. My eyes felt as though they were full of sharp bits of gravel. Everything seemed to be a kind of dull blur.

It was not long before they came for me. At seven o'clock two sentries opened the door of the cell. "Utinsky, here!" one said.

I was ready then and fairly calm. The other women could only watch me. We couldn't say anything to each other, but I knew what they thought, and they knew what I would want to say.

I walked down the corridor, telling myself unbelievingly, "I am being taken off to die. I am no different from the others. It happened to that man last night. It can happen to me. There is nothing more to hope for."

I tried to keep my mind on little things, on the cracks in the floor, on the faces of people who watched me through the bars of their cells, on the right.

But we weren't going in the direction of the prison yard. We weren't going that way at all! We were winding through corridors that led in a direction in which I had never been before. I kept track of the windings. And we were going down narrow, worn steps to a lower level. Something new was up.

I was taken down a dark passageway to the door of a cell. They opened it and pushed me inside. Then I heard them going up the steps. This was the awful thing known as "Solitary."

I walked around my cell, a dark little hole about four feet square. The door was of iron and near the top was a little opening about five inches by ten. Even that was barred. The rest — just damp, cold stone walls and slimy floor. I had read about dungeons. Well, this was it.

In the other cell there had been human companionship, even if we could not speak; in the other cell I could at least see the day come and go. Here there was nothing but a pale glimmer of light from the corridor. No face but the sentry's. I could not even lie down in comfort. I'm not very tall, heaven knows, but even I cannot straighten out in a four-foot space.

I didn't need to worry about the sickening lugao here. There wasn't any. And there wasn't any water. Not for four days and nights. But there were other things — huge flying cockroaches that banged against my face. My nerves were so tense that every time one of the horrid things touched me my heart nearly burst out of my body. There were things that crawled. There were foul, dank smells that made my flesh creep. And every time steps came down the corridor, I wondered if they were on an errand of death for me.

There isn't much to do but think in a place like that and you don't dare begin to think out loud. That would mean your control was slipping. I thought about my work. I knew that was all right. Everything had stopped automatically the moment I was arrested. That had been prepared for long in advance, from the time when I began to realize that I was under suspicion. When the Japanese had come for me at the hospital, I had bent over the bed of my patient and whispered, "They have come for me."

"Where?" she asked.

"Fort Santiago, I think. When I am gone, get word to Ernest Johnson."

Ernest Johnson was a patient in the hospital and my patient, who was a member of the organization, got a message to him. He sent word to Sparkplug, who bribed a man in the City Hall to hide the record of my marriage certificate. which showed I was an American, and then went to see Mrs. Yearsley.

Mrs. Robert Yearsley was an American woman who had escaped internment because she was stone blind, and her husband remained free to look after her. Her son, Robin, however, was a prisoner in Cabanatuan. We had long before worked out a plan by which we sent messages back and forth; she sent money to her son and I brought her his letters. Whenever I was sending supplies to Cabanatuan, I would telephone that I wanted a recipe for a cake. She would send her Filipino boy to me with money. When I got Robin's answer, I would telephone to say that I had made the cake.

Sparkplug went to Mrs. Yearsley with word that I had been arrested and she sent her Filipino to Cabanatuan to get in touch with Colonel Mack and say, "Stop everything."

Later, Colonel Mack told me that when the message came, they were so afraid that the truth about the smuggling would come out that they all ran around like ground squirrels burying stuff, money, notes, anything they might have in their possession. In the excitement, he said, he buried fifty pesos and never did find it again.

It was a comfort, of course, to know that no member of the organization was running into danger, but it was maddening to think that all these weeks of my imprisonment no food or medicine had been going into Cabanatuan. But there was no use in fretting about it. There was nothing I could do now.

I had mapped in my mind the course we followed in reaching this dungeon cell, so I knew where I was. If those dripping gray walls could have melted, I would be looking through the opening right down the street where I lived. I would be seeing, farther away, the roof of the High Commissioner's palace. I would see the University Club, Army and Navy Club, and Elks Club. I would see my own apartment.

It was like remembering something from another life, so remote, so detached from this cell that it had almost no relation to me at all.

I suppose at a time like that, shut away in solitary confinement, one is supposed to do some really constructive thinking. I didn't. You don't think much when every inch of your body seems to have a separate pain. You don't think much when you are frightened, expecting with every footstep you hear that something is going to happen to you. I was a little light-headed, but that was because I was running a temperature. Gangrene had set in on one leg by then. Thoughts came and went and drifted like smoke. I prayed a lot, too. Not so much that I would get out — though the hope was always there — but that I could be strong enough to hold out.

They probably were not orthodox prayers. I had never been a very religious person. If there was one thing I had had too much of, it was baptism. I must have had Original Sin sticking out all over me, because every one of my relatives had had me baptized: Baptist, Methodist, Lutheran — there were others I have forgotten now. One of the ministers practically drowned me. He ducked me under and, when I came up, he pounced on me, pushed me under and held me down. Maybe he was trying to drown the devil in me. It wasn't until I came out of prison that I joined a church of my own volition. Then I became a Catholic.

Once the sentry came to the door and looked in through the little opening. I don't know why they kept a sentry around. I could no more have gotten out of that place than a dead sardine could climb out of its can. But he hung around. This time he called, "Why you here?"

"I don't know."

"You do know," he persisted. "Why you here?"

"I guess they put me here because they think I am an American."

He laughed. "You not American. I am American."

He was, too! He had been born in the United States. His father was an American, his mother a Japanese. His whole family — that is, the ones who were too young to fight — were in the United States. The others were here in the Japanese service.

How I hated him! Yes, and all like him, for there were far too many of them who had used my country to get all they could and now were betraying it, torturing and killing its people.

He had two brothers, he said. One of them was a boxer who had won several titles. Both of them, he added proudly, were in the Japanese service.

Almost boiling with anger, I remembered that one of the Japanese who tortured me most was a man who told me he had lived in the United States for more than twenty years and raised a family there. One of his sons had come back to fight for Japan.

Then there was the interpreter who had raised a family in San Francisco. He used to watch for the mail which came in just before the daily questioning. Once I asked him, "Mail from home?"

"Yes," he replied. "Some good news, some bad." That was a lot for a Jap to acknowledge. His sister, who was a nurse, had studied in the United States. Yes, I raged inwardly, she is now helping Japanese get well to kill more Americans, helpless in places like this.

Perhaps I should try to forget, try to remember that the Japanese are human too. But I've seen too many fine, upstanding Americans reduced to ragged, dirty, starved slaves.

Some of them were just babies. Some of them were men of sixty, fine officers in the finest army in the world. Some of them were like the priests in the prison, emptying the slops of their fellow prisoners. No, I won't forget in a hurry.

All these thoughts had plenty of time to ferment in my mind during those hours in the dungeon cell. And then, on the fourth day, the door opened. All my old fears swarmed back. What now? The prison yard and a firing squad?

We were going back the way we had come. At least, it wasn't the graveyard. Whatever lay ahead, I was grateful in every inch of my body, in every part of my mind and heart, that I was walking again, that I was free of those clammy gray walls, of the iron door, of the roaches that slapped into my face, or squashed with a nauseating sound under my bare feet. But what now?

They took me to a different room this time. There were new officers and a new interpreter who asked me if I was willing to sign a paper pledging myself never to do anything against the Japanese Government. I said yes.

"Then," he said, "I have good news for you. This officer is to give you your freedom." The officer grinned like a billy goat.

They handed me a paper and I signed it. One sentence I still remember; "Since I have been in Fort Santiago for questioning, I have received courteous treatment from all officers and sentries and been provided with good food."

Escape to the Hills

I WALKED out of Fort Santiago, weaving with fatigue and relief. There was no escort. They just let me go. But at the gate the sentry halted me and I waited, my heart thumping, while he telephoned to see whether I had really been released.

Once in the walled city I lost my way and came out the wrong gate in the surrounding wall. Dizzy and bewildered, I fell flat in a great patch of saw-edged long grass and lay there for a long time unable to move. When I finally tried to get up, I discovered that I could not stand; I could not pull myself farther than my knees. There was nothing to do but wait until help of some kind came along.

After what seemed to be hours a Filipino rode by with a sidecar bicycle and I hailed him. He sat there, looking at me stupidly.

"You are an American, ma'am," he said. "You are an American. Where have you been?"

"It doesn't matter where I've been," I snapped. "Get me into that sidecar and take me home."

So he lifted me up, hoisted me into the sidecar and drove me home. He took me upstairs and Maria, my Filipina maid, after one look at me, burst into tears. I was filthy beyond description. For thirty-two days I had not washed or combed my hair. My white uniform had been slept in; it was ripped from the beatings and spattered with blood. Maria helped me to the heaven of a bath with soap and warm water and a hasty attempt to disinfect all my wounds. But it was a hopeless job. She took me to the hospital.

I was a mess. There was a large gangrenous area on my right leg and amputation was clearly indicated. All my organs had fallen from that month of terrific beatings over my back and I needed a major operation to put them back into place again. It seemed to me that all I wanted was decent food and water and to lie down in a clean bed with sheets, free of pain and able to rest without any struggle. But that wasn't possible. In the first place, I was going to make a fight for that leg, and the Filipino doctor reluctantly agreed to take a chance on treating the gangrenous area. In the second place, I dared not take ether for an operation. Heaven knows what I might say under ether, and the Japs weren't through with me yet. They'd never be through with me. So I decided on a spinal anesthetic.

Unfortunately for me, they miscalculated, and the effect of the spinal wore oft three-quarters of an hour before the operation was finished. For some reason, too, the effect of the spinal was one of partial paralysis. For days my hands were clenched and my face and muscles drawn and twisted.

For the next week, my fever soared skyhigh and I kept dreaming about sticks jabbing at my wounds. I would come out of a nightmare to find the doctor watching me anxiously. Hadn't I better have the leg amputated? No, I said grimly. What good was a nurse with one leg? And sure enough, in nine days the fever began to subside, the pain to become bearable and then gradually to fade away.

I was in the hospital for six weeks but at the end of that time I still had my leg, even though today there are ugly blue scars that have never disappeared. I'll carry them with me all my life. And three times a week, two of the Japanese officers who had beaten me came to sit in my room for an hour. They did not say anything. They just sat there silently and looked at me. Don't talk, their presence meant. We can take you again when we want you. And I said nothing about how I had got my infected legs and my damaged back. And the doctor wisely didn't ask.

A message reached me in the hospital which did a lot to hearten me. It told how, in Cabanatuan, Colonel Mack, hearing of my imprisonment at Fort Santiago, had asked 6,000 Americans to pause in silent prayer for me each day. Even gangrene seemed worthwhile then.

Of course, I went straight back to smuggling again, starting the life-saving supplies moving to Cabanatuan. One day, shortly after I got out of the hospital, a woman came running down the street toward me, a white woman whom I had never seen before. She was an American Jewess, who had married a Filipino named Soriano, who was mayor of a little town called Orion, near where Colonel Boone and the guerrilla forces were.

We had a long talk. Both she and her husband were acquainted with the inside of a Jap prison. They hadn't liked Soriano's lack of enthusiasm for the "Liberation." But the Japs had released them both and that was a tactical error on their part, for he had become a captain in the guerrilla forces and he was raising hell for the Japs.

His wife said he wanted to meet me and the next time he managed to slip into Manila he came to see me. "When you know you are going to be taken," he said, "come to us." He told me how to do it. When he went back, he told Colonel Boone about me and I managed to send supplies to

Boone and in return I got a receipt for them, met his wife who was in Manila and went with her when her baby was baptized.

About this time, too, one of the members of my organization was picked up by the Japanese for questioning and taken to Fort Santiago. She was an American girl who had married a Filipino. Her husband worked on a steamship line and he had been away on a trip when the war broke out, so he was unable to get back to the Islands. She had come to me in 1943, asking me to look up the name of a prisoner for her. Then one night she brought me fifty pesos to send to a soldier, and later began helping me to collect money. She had a four-year-old mestizo baby, Dian, and because there was no place for her to go, I took Dian, the best baby I ever saw, gentle, obedient, and dark brown.

The Apostolic Delegate of Manila knew of my work and he knew that the priests at Malate Convent were helping me. He approved because he knew it to be a true mission of mercy and succor. People of his faith had died in such work for generations. A young Filipino boy who belonged to his church was spying for the Apostolic Delegate while working for the Japanese at Fort Santiago. One night he appeared in great excitement. He had found a list. On it were the names of Father Lalor, Father Kelly, Father Joseph Monaghan, Father John Henaghan — and Miss U.

It was early morning when a summons came from Father Lalor. The Japanese were after me. I was to be picked up. The time had come for me to escape to the hills. I scurried around getting ready, trying to keep the baby from being scared. But she balked at leaving behind a small yellow kitten which I had taken in because it was lost and hungry. The only way to keep her quiet was to take along that damned cat. So I set off with a brown baby and a yellow kitten on the greatest adventure of my life.

Two hours after I left my apartment the Japanese came for me. From that moment on there was a Japanese guard stationed there, waiting for my return. There was one in my apartment the day an American plane flew over and blew it to bits with a bomb.

When I reached the Malate Convent, Father Lalor, Father Kelly, Fathers Monaghan, Henaghan and Father Peter Fallon, and an Irish boy named Jack Sullivan, were busy loading a carretela with medical supplies for the guerrillas, for I did not intend to go to them empty-handed when their need was so great. The priests had also gathered all the food they could scrape together and all the clothes they could find. They even remembered to pack some books, for which later I said prayers of thanks.

They looked up without surprise when I put in an appearance, complete with brown baby and kitten. After all, they had worked with me for almost three years. If I had come in dragging a young python by the tail, they would have survived it.

Lee was waiting for me. Captain Soriano's instructions had been: "When the word comes that the Japs are after you, go to Banca Side (a docking space for small boats on the Pasig River, which opens out into Manila Bay). You will find boats there with Filipino fishermen. Take a Filipino with you to do the talking and arrange your passage, for these boatmen have licenses to carry passengers and some cargo. They should charge you about fifty pesos. They are our men.

"Take the banca (a small rowboat) to Orion. When you get there, do not talk to any adults and do not ask for me by name. Wait until you see a child and then say, 'American Boy,' which is my code name. If he belongs to the guerrillas, he will know what to do. If he does not, he won't know what you are talking about anyhow, so no harm will be done."

There were to be no written messages. One slip there and the whole work would collapse like a balloon. Worse, every member of the guerrillas would, in the favorite phrase of the Japanese, find his belly full of bayonet. So I had to memorize every detail of my instructions. Fortunately the Japs can't see inside a brain.

Lee was waiting at the Convent, as I expected. Some way or other, Lee would get me safely on a banca unless he had a Jap bullet in his heart.

But even Lee set up a howl when he saw the three of us. "No, no, Miss Peggy. Not to Banca Side with baby and cat. Very danger. Miss Peggy. They see you leave house and all time Japs look for a white woman, brown baby, yellow cat."

But Lee was going to get us safely to Banca Side. He had himself a job, but he figured it out. He took Dian and the kitten. He reasoned that the Japs would not suspect a Chinese with a baby. He could go through Manila to the river unchallenged, and off he set.

Meanwhile, the priests had finished loading the supplies in the carretela and found a Filipino boy to serve as interpreter. The cochero and the box of books were in the front seat and I sat on the back seat — boards laid across the body — surrounded by sacks of clothing in which the food and medical supplies were hidden — with the Filipino interpreter beside me.

I said goodbye then to the priests of Malate Convent. I never saw them again. Whether or not their names appeared on the Jap death lists, they refused to escape and stayed behind to do the work they had set themselves to do. So the Japs caught them and killed them, shot, crucified, burned them to death.

I didn't know that then. I waved goodbye and jogged off in the little carretela, on my way at last to the guerrillas in the hills. The Japs didn't pay much attention to Filipinos driving little cartloads of stuff. They were always going up and down the roads, especially since they had been "liberated." We weren't even stopped until we had nearly reached the river bank. Then a couple of sentries jumped on the sides of the cart. "Where you go?"

I didn't open my mouth. I shook my head, fiddled with the packages and finally opened the box of books. They chattered and poked at the books and I showed them the clothes, hoping they would not reach into the sacks and find the medicine. They let us go.

Lee was waiting on the river bank, his face wrinkled with worry, "Miss Peggy," he said, "no banca for Orion till afternoon. Too danger you wait here."

He scouted around a bit and found a lumberyard near the landing place which would be a good place, for us to hide in until evening. By then he was sure there would be a banca.

I wouldn't pick out a lumberyard to set up housekeeping in but it was a lot better than Fort Santiago, so Dian and I and the kitten hid there while Lee kept a weather eye out at the landing place, looking for a banca. Every so often he would slip back with food that he had managed to get in some way, and water for Dian. And once he came up beaming, with a fishhead for the kitten.

We didn't dare spend the night in the lumberyard, even though Lee could forage food for us. It was much too risky. If we couldn't get a banca to Orion, we would have to get one going nearby and take a chance on getting the rest of the way. The Filipino interpreter finally made arrangements for us to be taken to Abucay, a barrio near Orion, where, the boatman promised faithfully, we would find a banca to take us the rest of the way.

The boat we finally got was not a banca but a batel, a long sailboat, with four oarsmen on either side, and room for fifty people. I wasn't happy about it because the fewer people who saw me escape from Manila, the better I liked it. But there seemed to be no choice.

"Better go. Miss Peggy," Lee said. "Very, very danger here." It was a good thing that he could not see ahead to the next few hours or there would have been a whitehaired Chinese in Manila.

The three of us got into the boat. My sacks and the box of books were piled around us and covered with a tarpaulin. There was no shelter for the passengers. The boatman sat, or rather lived, in the middle of the boat, where he had a charcoal stove on which rice was cooking. The other passengers piled in, all Filipinos, and the batel moved out and down the river. Lee stood on the bank and watched us go. It was a long, long time before I found him again.

It was about the middle of the afternoon when the batel started across the bay. That meant it would be night before we landed near Abucay. I didn't like that. In the first place, I wasn't sure of the passengers. It had been easy to get this far. I wondered if it had been too easy.

I watched the passengers and I knew they were watching me too. There was no use fooling myself. They might easily be collaborators. They were probably wondering whether I was. One passenger in particular was taking a decided interest in me, and at length he moved forward so he could talk to the boatman. I heard them muttering together in Tagalog. By this time anything like that had me bristling with suspicion.

The afternoon dragged along. My uneasiness about the passengers had quieted down, all except that one. He was a Filipino from Manila and there was always a possibility that he might know who I was.

At last it was evening and the sky was full of gloomy clouds. Darkness always comes fast in the tropics, but this time it came faster. While it was daylight I could watch the other passengers, but in the dark I could only guess at what they were doing.

Quite late it began to rain. We sat there, growing wetter and more miserable every minute. I could see the rain making little pits in the dark water. I protected Dian as well as I could from the rain, and now and then I dozed. Then I was awakened by a faint humming that grew to a roar. Airplanes! At first I was tremendously thrilled. At last! At last! The Yanks had come back to bomb Manila. I felt like screaming out my triumph. Then I remembered that the batel, tossing about in the bay, was a pretty helpless target. The Yanks were on the march again and that was swell, but I did not want to be killed by a Yank bomb. That would really be too much. The Americans were bombing military installations near Manila, barracks, and passing boats. And darned if I wasn't right in the middle of it!

At length the planes moved on and I fell asleep, jerking awake now and then when a waterfall ran down my neck. The batel was twisting around through a kind of bayou dotted with little islands just big enough to hold a clump of palms or mangroves. The boat shifted and turned. At length it stopped at a landing place and most of the passengers got off, including the one who had taken such a persistent interest in me. I felt better then, but not for long.

I was just getting ready to climb from the batel into a banca when the boatman stopped me. "You will stay here," he said peremptorily. "You will not get off the boat."

I protested but it did no good. I was in no spot for bargaining. I did not know what was wrong. Rain-soaked and bone-tired, I just sat down to wait, holding Dian.

Then there was the sound of oars and a banca drew alongside. There were half a dozen Filipinos in it and one of them was the man who had watched me. The banca had come for me and I was to get in. I was not to take my things, which were to stay on the batel.

They must not find the drugs. How was I to explain them? Automatically I began to make up stories. I had come to nurse sick Filipinos. But how was I to account for procuring the practically unobtainable drugs? Well, one thing at a time.

I turned to the boatman. "You are responsible for these things," I said fiercely. "If I can't take them with me, you'll have to look out for them yourself."

Then I climbed into the banca with Dian. I didn't know where I was going. I didn't know why. And I was scared to death. I was the only white woman for miles around.

We reached a landing place and began an hour's march through a bamboo forest, a heavy slogging through rain-soaked, slippery trails, where the footing was uncertain and all of us slithered over brush and debris. For once in my life I was just plain sorry for myself. What was the use, I thought, in escaping execution in Manila if I was going to lose my head here? No one would ever find me in this place. If I had been killed in Manila, somebody would find out. People I knew would come looking for me. But no one knew I was here. Then I'd slip on the path and have to pick myself up and get going again. I got mad then instead of sorry and started to swear.

At last we came to a narrow bamboo bridge, just a plank across a stream where we could cross only single file. My escorts were the most villainous specimens I ever saw and I thought my time had come. Nobody who looked like that could possibly be a friend. We began to pass native huts and when I saw that a man was stationed at the corner of each of them, I didn't feel any better.

By this time I had a procession. They were armed with the most threatening looking array of rifles, bayonets and side arms I'd come across. As we went along, the guards, one after another, fell into line, and if any of them looked more vicious than the last, it was the one who finally halted us at a bamboo hut.

The hut was lighted by a burning rag floating in a tin can of coconut oil and set at the edge of the table. The only other furniture was a rickety chair. One of the men drew the chair up to the table and told me to sit down so the light shone directly on my face. My questioner stood in the shadow.

By this time I knew all the mechanics of being on the wrong end of a questioning detail. I ought to. It wasn't the questions that bothered me. It was the answers. I knew a lot of answers but the trouble was that I didn't know which ones to use.

Your papers? I handed them over. What are you doing here? I've come to look after the sick Filipinos in the mountains. No work for you in Manila?

I made up my mind and plunged. "I was afraid the Americans would come to Manila. It is safer for me here."

He shot a look at me. "Once someone heard you say in Manila, 'Here come the devils,' when the Japs walked by. Is that true?"

Where did they get that? What did they know about me? "Well," I said easily, "anybody can make a mistake. That's why they put erasers on pencils."

"It says here you are a Lithuanian."

"Yes," I said, "that's almost the same as German."

That tore it. His face stiffened. "That's what we thought. We ought to take you out and shoot you."

Those were lovely words. All at once my heart was light again. I'd fallen in with the guerrillas! I looked around again at those armed men and darned if I hadn't smuggled most of those guns to them myself.

"Now let me ask you some questions," I said, sitting up straight. "Do you know Colonel Boone?"

"Do you?" he countered.

"Not personally," I admitted. "But I know his wife."

"What's her name?"

"Millie." He nodded and I clinched it. "I was with her when her baby was baptized. Do you know Colonel Boone's signature?" Out of the hem of my skirt I ripped Colonel Boone's letter and handed it to him.

"That's enough," said the guerrilla, and he grinned.

Enough? It was almost too much. Back to the landing place we went to get my supplies from the batel. When we got there my heart sank, for the batel had gone. However, we found all my precious drugs carefully stacked in a nearby hut. The guerrillas got me a banca to take me to Orion. At this point I did not want to go on. There were planes over the bay and from the noise, their target seemed to be near Orion. However, I had no choice, so I climbed in with little Dian and the kitten.

Within a few hours we reached Orion. Then we saw what the bombing had been about. The Japs had mounted machine guns on a grounded cargo ship and an American plane had come to blast it. The Japs had shot down the plane and they were hunting for the bodies. During the excitement our banca slipped into shore, right beside the cargo ship.

I jumped out of the banca, slipped, fell and broke a bone in my foot! Like a fool I started to cry. A native boy came up and stared at me open-mouthed.

"American Boy?" I asked.

The boy turned and ran like a deer. In a few moments I heard the sound of running feet. I looked up and saw Captain Soriano racing toward me, wearing red fisherman's pants, his shirttail flapping as he came. And there I lay in a heap, practically in touching distance of the Jap cargo ship, clutching the brown baby and the yellow kitten. And no camera nearer than Manila! They do these things a lot better in the movies. I stopped crying and began to laugh.

Guerrilla Nurse

I COULD NOT be left lying on the beach, in full sight of the Japanese cargo ship, and I could not walk with that broken bone in my foot. Captain Soriano sent for some men who picked me up and ran at top speed with me to an old church where I could be hidden safely for the night and, if need be, for several days.

Father Lopez Pascual, the Filipino priest in charge of the church, carried on his priestly duties in Orion during the day, and at night removed his robes and, dressed like any Filipino peasant, went about his hazardous work as a contact man for the guerrillas.

The church was very old and attached to it was a convent with huge, drafty rooms. Father Pascual gave Dian and me a room on the upper floor of the convent and brought me a charcoal burner so that I could cook our food. All the supplies and drugs I had brought with me were stacked in another room, ready to be conveyed to the guerrillas.

When I was settled for the night, Father Pascual slipped out of the convent and went about his business. He offered me no information and I asked him no questions. Before he left he said, "Some of the guerrillas will be through in a night or two." (They always traveled by night, of course.) "You can send word to Colonel Boone by a runner that you are here." And he was gone.

The convent was empty except for Dian and me. I could not run if I had to. I didn't know what lay ahead. But at least it was freedom and a chance to be useful, and beyond that I did not care much.

The night before, I had slept only fitfully, what with the rain and the bombings going on all around me, but that night I slept, making up for lost time. A nurse learns to sleep when she has the opportunity, to husband her strength as much as possible, both of which lessons had served me well in prison. They were to serve me better in the months that lay ahead. For if I had worried when I lay down at night whether I'd be alive in the morning, there would not have been much sleep for me.

At midnight the following night the priest signaled. "Hendry is here," he told me.

Two boys came up the stairs: Warren Hendry, an American soldier, and young Peter Seekts, an English mestizo, both members of the guerrilla forces, and both incredibly young. On the chance that they might arrive that night, I had cooked a lot of beans and the three of us ate and talked all through the night.

The guerrillas at that time knew little of what was happening in Manila and even less of what was happening outside the Philippines. I told them all I could remember of the news we had gathered over the short-wave radio and described the rapid advance of the Yanks. It couldn't be long now. It simply couldn't. MacArthur was keeping his word. He was coming back.

In exchange, the two boys told me what the guerrilla forces were like and explained something of guerrilla fighting. This was not an army like other armies, with uniforms and proper equipment. It was made up of a few Americans who had escaped the March of Death or had got away from prison camps; of people who had slipped out of Manila to take a part in the war against the Japs; of Filipinos, and of Negritoes — a small black people similar to the African pygmies. Their uniforms consisted of anything in the nature of clothing they could find, and for many of them that meant nothing but a G-string. Their weapons were guns that had been smuggled to them or those they had taken from the Japanese. Their food — when they had any — was whatever they could manage to forage for themselves.

Yet the guerrillas were killing ten Japanese for every one of their own men who died. They had learned to fight like animals or like devils. And when they were captured, they died without revealing anything they knew.

For a long time I had realized that sooner or later I would end by working with the guerrillas in the hills, with the rest of those who had defied the Japanese and had been lucky to get away with it. And I do mean lucky. The guerrillas are given a great deal of credit and, heaven knows, I don't grudge it to them. I lived with them and fought with them, I ran with them when the Japs were too close behind and bound up their wounds when they were injured. Part of the time we slept on the ground in damp coffee patches; we were close to starvation most of the time and we were frightened all the time.

But even that was heaven compared with being behind the barbed wire with the prisoners who, when they were not forced into slave labor, when they were not ill, when they were not tortured, ate their hearts out in inaction.

I have been on both sides of the fence, in and out of prison, and I have fought with the guerrillas, and there is no doubt in my mind that they have the best of it. They had the most essential thing — the possibility of choice. For, after all, if they fought and ran and starved and got scared half to death, they asked for it. The guerrilla was strictly a volunteer.

When Warren Hendry and Peter Seekts got ready to return, I wrote a letter to Colonel John P. Boone of the guerrilla forces, telling him what had happened in Manila and explaining that I had had to escape to the hills. I told him too, that I had come with as many drugs and supplies as I was able to bring.

The boys set off for Boone's camp and I waited for another three days. It was about midnight of the third day that I heard feet shuffling on the floor below me. It sounded like a whole regiment. My heart was in my mouth until a voice called softly, "Miss U, Colonel Boone has sent for you."

They came up then, as I still could not walk. There were twenty-eight men in the convoy that was to take me and my stuff up to the hills. In charge of the convoy was Valencia, the guerrilla who had captured me and threatened to have me shot.

There was no time to waste, so the men loaded my stuff on their shoulders and put me, with Dian and the kitten, in a bamboo chair they had rigged up on poles, so that I could be carried.

All that night we moved through the bamboo forest, climbing most of the time. It was pitch-dark. All around me I could hear men walking softly but I could see nothing. No one dared strike a light.

I sat in the bamboo chair, holding the sleeping baby, and wondering how on earth this had happened to me. Wondering how on earth Peggy Doolin had turned into the notorious Miss U, the only white woman in God knows how many miles, escaping for her life through a bamboo forest.

At daylight the men around me began to take shape as shadows and then they became Filipinos, tired and dirty and ragged, plodding wearily ahead, shifting my boxes from one pair of aching shoulders to another, changing carriers for my bamboo chair.

That night it rained heavily and we stopped at a bamboo hut. The roof was like a sieve and the water poured in. There was hardly a dry inch of space. I lay on the floor, wet and hungry, with some twenty Filipinos lying all around me, their clothes steaming, the smell of their unwashed bodies heavy in the air, their chorus of snores making the night hideous. And I slept.

It took us two days and two nights to climb up into the hills to Tala Ridge, where Lieutenant Colonel Victor Abad, a Filipino, was in command of the Second Regiment of guerrillas.

Not long before, there had been a sugar cane mill on Tala Ridge, but the Japanese suspected the owner of helping the guerrillas. They cut off his head and burned his mill. There was nothing left now but the cane patch and a little house set up high on long poles, with floors of split bamboo and walls of sawali — a woven split bamboo — and a roof of nipa grass.

I was carried up the steep ladder into a spotless little room with a charcoal burner in the center, on which pots of food were cooking. The wife of the murdered mill owner still lived there and the place had become a headquarters for guerrillas.

Colonel Abad shook hands with me. "We need you here," he said. "We need you badly."

At first I did not hear him. I was looking out of the hut, seeing something I could hardly believe, something so beautiful my eyes stung with tears. Coming toward me slowly, across the parade ground, was the American flag. It was the first time I had seen it fly since it was lowered in Manila.

"We need you," Abad repeated patiently. "Many of my regiment are sick or wounded."

"All right," I said. "Bring them on."

I sat on the floor with a tin first-aid kit beside me, and Abad brought in my patients. I took care of everything that came up, giving typhoid and paratyphoid injections, bandaging gunshot wounds, treating dysentery and hideous ulcers. All around me Filipino guerrillas were lying on the floor, resting, their guns within reach of their hands, and little Negritoes squatted beside them, holding the bows and arrows with which they are so deadly.

There was a Filipina girl whom I had taught to make a record of each patient, the name, the address — if any — what I had given, and what the treatment should be, so that someone could carry on when I was gone.

While I was in the midst of my primitive nursing, there was an outbreak of gunshots. Valencia gave orders that I was to be carried out into the cane patch. Two Filipinos picked me up, took me down the ladder, and ran out into the cane. The convoy scattered with the guerrillas who had been rounded up for treatment.

We lay on our faces in the cane. It was swelteringly hot. Bugs crawled over my neck and my face, over my arms and legs. I have always loathed crawling things, but they are worse when you are afraid to move to brush them off.

Then there was a rustling sound and I turned around. A beaming Filipino was crouching beside me. He had grabbed the two big pots which were cooking in the hut, one filled with mongo beans and the other with rice. In guerrilla fighting you don't waste food.

We lay on our bellies in the cane patch while the Filipino scooped out the beans and rice and served them to us on banana leaves. We broke off pieces of cane to use for spoons. So we ate while the shooting went on and on.

A long time later, the signal came for us to return to the hut. In a few minutes, a runner came up with a note.

"Stop shooting," it read. "I have 200 armed men." There was no signature.

Valencia had only forty men all told. "Lay your arms down," he replied. "I also have 200 armed men." He handed the note to a runner.

What next, I wondered, peering out of the hut. There were two men coming over the hill and one of them was waving his hat. I looked a second time — Warren Hendry and Peter Seekts.

They came up the ladder, grinning. "Where are your 200 armed men?" they asked Valencia, and laughed.

Valencia was angry. "Did you write that note?"

Hendry nodded. "We heard all the shooting," he explained, "and we thought you were Japanese. Peter and I decided to try a bluff so we sent you that note. Then when your reply came back, we asked the runner what your people looked like.

"He said, 'There is a white woman there. She must be a doctor. She's got bandages on everyone!'"

"'That's Miss U,' we said, so we came on up."

And after all the excitement, it turned out that the firing had simply been another bunch of guerrillas doing some target practice!

The next day, the convoy carried me on toward Boone's headquarters. We were within two kilometers of it when we saw a typhoon coming up, so the convoy left me at an outpost and went back, sending a runner on to Colonel Boone.

At two o'clock in the morning he arrived. He was a young man, about thirty-four, with reddish brown hair, blue eyes, a pleasant personality. In the regular Army he had been a buck private, though he was a man of education and a born leader.

He held out his hand. "Thank God for you. Miss U," he said. "You are needed here."

We talked for a little while and then he went back to headquarters. The following morning he sent for me and I was commissioned brevet second lieutenant in the guerrilla army.

At that time, most of the fighting was going on in the vicinity of Tala, where Colonel Abad's second regiment was, so Colonel Boone sent me back to Tala Ridge.

All the way back to Tala, riding the bamboo chair, holding the brown baby and that damned cat, I sat there answering salutes. The guerrillas might not have much in the way of uniforms, but they yielded to no one on ceremony. The men who passed me were barefooted; they were filthy; they were lousy — so was I by that time. But we all saluted.

Being a guerrilla nurse is like nothing else on earth. I was needed all right. In fact, I was the entire medical staff of the whole outfit. Before me there had been only a Filipino who, in spite of his willingness, knew nothing but a little first aid.

I found it was simpler to try to forget the things you learn in hospitals. Anyone in a well-conducted hospital would faint at the conditions under which I treated those men. I had to hospitalize my patients in bamboo huts which a few men could construct in a few hours and which, when the outpost sentry fired a warning shot, could be abandoned in a few minutes. Cots were made of improvised bamboo, we had practically no blankets, and the cracks in the huts let in swarming insects.

Colonel Abad gave me a little hut to live in and set up a tiny shelter some distance away for a clinic. No one was allowed to come to my hut for fear they would make a trail which might lead the Japanese to me.

There was no pampering of patients. There were cases of malaria, dysentery, and tropical ulcers — those gnawing sores that eat right down to the bone. Every day they had to be cleaned out with weak permanganate and boric, and dressed with sulfa. There was one half-white Filipino who kept on fighting, wading in swamp mud, with six inches of his shinbone laid open by such an ulcer.

Guerrilla fighting is like that, and as for guerrilla nursing, all you can do is give the indicated medicine — if you have it — and trust in God. Sometimes you can't even do that much. When I escaped from Manila, all

I had with me was 44 c.c. of anti-tetanus toxoid, and every gunshot wound calls for three injections of one c.c. each.

Of course, we were able to replenish the supply from time to time. Once a week, runners, taking the same route I had taken, slipped into Manila and went to Father Lalor. And the good father went in search of the drugs. There was a Chinese druggist, Don Louis Teehankee, who never disappointed us and often gave us huge boxes of supplies, as well as cash. He was once taken to Fort Santiago and his father, a doctor, was killed on the street, sometime in 1943. I had gone to him myself, in fear and trembling lest he turn me in. I would never have dared to go if our need had not been so much greater than the safety of any one person. But he had given me an immense amount of drugs, and ever since then he had turned over to us all that he could manage to give us.

Guerilla nursing would have been greatly simplified if we could ever have remained in one spot. But in the first thirty days, we struck camp twenty times. We'd move on a little way, put up some more huts for our patients and carry on the best we could.

It is surprising, indeed, how much nursing got done in those little ramshackle huts. Whenever we stopped anywhere long enough, I taught willing native girls about first aid so that they could carry on in some way and keep records of what had been given each man. But we seldom stayed in one place more than a few days. Either the Japanese would get too close or the guerrillas would be chasing them out of a barrio, and I followed the fighting as closely as I could. I still have records showing the malaria, gunshot wounds, fever and exhaustion cases I treated.

In spite of all this, I lost only one patient during my whole time in the hills, a Filipino boy who died of dysentery. I kept him isolated in a shack to prevent contagion and stayed with him to the end.

No patient got much attention, however. There were 200 men to look after and there was only one of me. People talk of "the lady with a lamp." I was the lady with a .45. My methods were crude, but so were the conditions.

Some ten days after I settled down at my clinic at Tala, there was a battle between the Japanese and the guerrillas.

The next morning Abad came in, bringing me a lot of patients with gunshot wounds and barbed-wire cuts. I got some Filipinos to start a fire and sterilize needles.

I had just started an anti-tetanus injection, when a Filipina woman came running down the hill, yelling, "Japs!"

My patient leaped to his feet.

"You come back here," I told him.

"Me fight," he shouted.

"Me shoot," I said grimly, and he sat down and got his injection. I was not going to waste that medicine.

Then we tore down into the riverbed. By that time, of course, I could walk again. One of the guerrillas picked up Dian and I gathered into my dress all the drugs I could carry. But I made the worst mistake of my life. The Japanese were so close that in my excitement I forgot my shoes.

Down in the riverbed they hid Dian and me in a big hollow tree. We crouched there for hours, listening to the whine of bullets, to shouts and screams. I was close to tears. It seemed no use. You bandaged men up and took care of their wounds and shot medicine into them, and what good did it do? Here I hid in a tree, and up there my men were probably getting themselves killed.

Dian lay in my arms and didn't make a sound. She just stroked the kitten and waited. Everyone was afraid of Dian at first, because a baby who cried at the wrong moment would endanger everyone. But Dian learned early. She never made a sound.

Whenever we heard a warning shot or got a command to move, I would say, "Come on, Honey, we've got to go."

"Japanese!" she would whisper, and come quietly.

We had been in the hollow tree for hours when we heard soft whistling. Colonel Abad and an American guerrilla. Major Romaine, were looking for us. They had brought us some duck eggs they had salvaged from somewhere.

When we got back, the camp was gone. The Japanese had burned everything. And worst of all, they had taken my shoes.

All that night, I marched barefooted through the bamboo forest. It was pitch-dark and I held on to the man nearest me. It did not help any to know the Japanese had been through here only a few hours earlier.

We had walked ten miles by daylight when we reached another camp, but almost before we got settled, the Japanese raided us and we had to move on again.

We were always moving. I waded rivers with the water up to my shoulders, hanging on to the stirrup of a horse while some Filipino carried

Dian on his shoulders. I came into little evacuated barrios at nightfall and lay on the floor, my clothing wet and muddy, and hungry, always hungry. Often enough someone would break open a coconut and my ration of food for the day would be a square inch of coconut. We were — all of us — half starved all the time.

The whole outfit was Dian's devoted slaves. If any guerrilla got hold of a horse, she rode on the march. Otherwise she was carried on someone's shoulder. The men ran around trying to find eggs for her and an occasional chicken. When any carabao of the right sex happened along, it was laid under contribution for a ketchup bottle of milk, which has a fine flavor and is even richer than cow's milk.

It was months since I had seen a white woman and as time passed, I looked less and less like one. When we were near a river I would bathe and wash my clothes, but I could not seem to do anything about the lice in my hair. My clothes wore down to rags and finally I had nothing but a kind of playsuit. Someone found me a pair of men's shoes that I stuffed with grass so I wouldn't lose them.

Though I had not seen a mirror, I could tell that I was skin and bone. In fact, I got so thin that I had to give up carrying a .45 and pack a .38 instead. I just wasn't heavy enough to manage the other one.

We got our food on the country, when we got any. When you are hungry enough, practically anything seems edible. For the most part, we ate vines and leaves, for there are plenty of those in the forest. I cooked them and they weren't so bad. But there was one fuzzy leaf that I cooked every way I could think of and it was still fuzzy. Swallowing it was like eating caterpillars.

Now and then the men killed and ate a monkey. Sometimes, the Negritoes would kill a wild boar with bow and arrow. Then they would run from one guerrilla camp to another, taking parts to the men. Boar is dark and strong-tasting, and it requires a lot of cooking.

I cooked it with papaya and at least it was nourishing.

Although we practically lived in coffee patches, we were unlucky with coffee. It was always either in bloom or green or gone.

If I had looked ahead, I never could have lived through those months. There are things you know beyond any question are impossible. The strange thing is that human beings learn to do the impossible if they have to. What helped most was the fact that I could not see ahead. At first, I lived from week to week, then from day to day, and finally from minute to minute.

We never knew when we took off our shoes whether we would ever put them on again. A man would go over the hill to get water and never come back. It was as easy as that. You get fatalistic about death when it is all around you. It is so close, it strikes so often, the chances are so poor, that you simply can't afford to do much worrying. You take things as they come, and if you are surprised sometimes to find you are still alive, you are glad to be living.

So the weeks passed and we played hide and seek with the Japanese, diving for cover when they came too close. My clothes dropped off with mildew and thorns, and I battled lockjaw and Hongkong foot. And it seemed little enough. Nothing would have been too much to do for men who fought and took risks like the guerrillas.

One night I was alone when I saw a group of men coming toward me, noiselessly, single file. I was afraid to look up. I saw their shoes — Japanese military footgear! I reached for my gun to fire a warning shot when the man at the head of the line spoke softly,

"I have a wounded man here, ma'am. Can you fix him?"

They lined up in front of me then, sixteen men in full Japanese uniform, with Japanese guns in their hands. The leader's name was Bondoc. His name in the guerrillas was Captain Magtangol. They had just been in a battle with the Japanese, he told me, and his fifteen men had killed nineteen Japanese and taken their equipment.

Magtangol shook his head apologetically. "One of my men was careless," he said. "He's got a bullet in his arm."

The Yanks Come Back!

There were separate guerrilla camps scattered all through the hills. Small groups had more mobility and there was less danger of the Japanese doing any extensive damage when they could meet only one small group at a time. In Colonel Boone's headquarters were Sergeant Fletcher, Sergeant William Gateley, Private James Boyd, Warren Hendry, Peter Seekts, and Francis Seekts. There was one camp of which Lieutenant Colonel Frank R. Lloyd, of the United States Army, was in charge. With him were Lieutenant Colonel Edgar Wright, Major Royal Reynolds, Jr., Major A. H. Romaine, and Captain Lester Chase. In another camp were Colonel Merrill, Lieutenant Colonel Peter D. Calyer, Major Roy Tuggles, and Private Carl W. Roy. In still another were Edwin P. Ramsey and Robert Lapham. The leaders of these camps held more or less regular meetings, at which they pooled their information and planned their campaigns. As time passed, and the Yanks moved from island to island up the Pacific in their seven-league boots, the meetings were more frequent in preparation for the landing. Around Thanksgiving, the Americans had reached Leyte and we were expecting an American landing at Lingayen Gulf at any time.

All this time, of course, I had been assigned to duty with the Filipino guerrilla forces under the command of Colonel Abad. It was becoming harder and harder to get the medical supplies I needed from Manila and to find enough food to keep up our strength. And then, just when it seemed to me that things could not possibly be more difficult, they got worse.

For some time we had been camping in a sunless, dank coffee patch near Tala, and Dian had come down with pneumonia. I was frantic because I knew that she would die if we remained in that unhealthful spot and I had almost nothing to work with in order to nurse her.

Dian was the best baby I ever saw. She was dark brown. When I first got her, I nearly scrubbed the skin off her. Up to that time, I had been critical of marriages between white men and native women, even when many of them turned out extraordinarily well. But after knowing Dian, and having her with me for so long a time, I understood it a lot better.

No authority on child care would ever recommend the kind of life Dian had to live, without shelter or sanitation or anything like sufficient food, and constantly in danger of her life. Yet she never cried and never complained. Lessons no baby should have to learn had been drilled into her.

Her fever got higher and higher and she lay quiet without a whimper. As usual we were quartered in an open bamboo hut. We dared not strike a match at night because we never knew how close the Japanese might be, and the light of a match can be seen for an incredible distance, particularly in a pitch-black jungle.

One night her condition became so serious that I thought she was going to die. Francis Seekts, who was always on hand when I needed him, worked with me to save the baby. Francis was Peter Seekts' brother. Not long after this he went to see his widowed mother and was caught and beheaded by the Japanese before his mother's eyes. He was just seventeen years old. He held up the blanket and cautiously struck a light while I bathed her in alcohol. But her fever climbed and climbed.

The next morning rain poured down and it was muddy and dank in the coffee patch. I was so mad that I could hardly see. I left Francis with the baby and marched up the hill, slithering and sliding through the mud, to Abad's headquarters. I was soaking wet when I got there and that did not improve my temper any. I gave Abad hell. If the baby died, I told him hotly, it would be his fault. She did not have a chance in that coffee patch. I wanted to go to Colonel Lloyd and I wanted to go now.

"You couldn't make it," Colonel Abad told me. "It's impossible."

"I'm accustomed to doing the impossible," I snapped.

Down the hill I marched again, still mad, dripping with rain so that I looked like a walking waterfall. Francis and I fixed Dian in a blanket and slung it between poles so that she could be carried with as little strain on her as possible. I wrapped her carefully to protect her from the rain and we went up the hill again to Abad.

By that time, night was coming on, but I was so worried and so furious that I was determined to go on to Colonel Lloyd's camp that night.

"You can't do it," Colonel Abad said.

"Why not?"

"Leeches."

He won. I would rather face a bunch of Japanese than a horde of hungry leeches any time. So we spent the night at Colonel Abad's camp and I was glad that we did, because that night I had a long talk with Sergeant Gateley, one of the guerrillas about whom I had heard. When he sat down beside me, I recognized him at once because part of his ear had been cut off.

After I had put Dian to sleep, we sat talking in whispers. Sergeant Gateley had escaped from Corregidor on a raft with about forty men who managed to slip away together. The Japanese caught them and put them in prison. Like the prisoners I had seen in the corridor outside my cell at Fort Santiago, the Japanese had beaten them now and then in those sudden rages of theirs. Then, when they were tired of beating them, they settled down to drink their nightly quota of saki passing it to the Americans.

The prisoners did not attempt to understand the curious Japanese psychology, but they watched and bided their time. One night when the saki was passed around, the Americans pretended to drink but passed on the bottle untouched. As a result, the Japanese guards kept drinking until they passed out.

Fourteen of the Americans succeeded in escaping that night and they started for the hills. Sergeant William Gateley and Sergeant Fletcher were together and when they felt they had covered enough ground to be safe they went into a little hut that had been evacuated and lay down to sleep. By good luck they had stolen a blanket which they wrapped around them.

While they were asleep, some Filipino collaborators happened to pass the hut and see them. At that time the Japanese were offering five pesos for every American who was turned in, and the Filipinos advanced on the sleeping Americans with their bolos.

It was the blanket that saved them from being cut to ribbons. Even so, before they could get to their feet, the two men had terrible cuts on their arms, Gateley's face was slashed open and part of one ear had been sliced off.

The two men fought off those armed Filipinos with their bare fists and when they had finally driven them away, they tore up their shirts to bind their wounds and stop the bleeding. After that, they managed to reach the guerrilla troops in the hills and they knew just how lucky they were.

Early the next morning, with ten or twelve men as a convoy, among them four Negritoes, we set off again, still carrying Dian in the blanket hung between two poles. We marched all day long and at sundown we came to Colonel Lloyd's camp, 2500 feet up in the hills.

It was not as easy as it sounds because we had to climb up and down two other mountains to reach the one on which Colonel Lloyd was encamped. One of my convoy, an elderly Negrito named Damacio, had been mayor of the Negrito tribe before the war. As no one took the risk of approaching a guerrilla camp unannounced, Damacio was sent ahead to tell them that we were coming.

Colonel Lloyd had a unique way of getting an alarm. Beside his hut he had a pole with a ketchup bottle stuck on the top. Nailed on the hut, beside the ketchup bottle, was a tin mess kit. A string ran down the pole and through the bushes so that anyone coming up the hill would trip over the string, which would pull the pole, making the ketchup bottle hit the mess kit with a plunk.

Damacio felt so important at convoying the only white woman in the hills that all he could say when he arrived was, "Senora blanca, pickaninny."

I came up the hill to see the funniest sight of my life.

Outside the hut, standing at the edge of the hill, two men were waiting to greet me. Their shoes were mended with the hides of wild boars, their clothes were patched with pieces of gunny sack. Reynolds had long curly whiskers, his hair hanging down to his shoulders, two front teeth broken off from eating com. Lloyd had dark brown whiskers clear down to his chest, and he was bent over because he was badly crippled with rheumatism.

They looked at me and I stood looking at them. "Well," I said at last, "have I got into the House of David?"

They took me into the hut. There were two bamboo cots and one bamboo chair. They pulled up the chair for me and got to work hospitably making tea with dried mango leaves. Major Reynolds heroically relinquished his cot to me and for all the remaining weeks until the Americans finally landed, he slept on the ground under it.

Up in the hills, Dian began to get well again. There was a tense feeling that something was about to happen. The Americans were dropping pamphlets now, telling the Filipinos to stay off the roads so there would be no congestion when they came in. And when the "holidays" came, they dropped Christmas cards!

It was not right, Colonel Lloyd insisted, for a child to have no playthings. So with a stick and supplies which he stole from my medicine kit — septic gauze for clothing, gentian violet for eyes, he turned out a doll that was the most important thing in Dian's life. It even replaced the kitten in her affections.

Almost daily the American bombing came closer and closer. At first Dian was frightened by the heavy explosions, as our fliers bombed Japanese convoys.

"It's all right," I told her. "Those are Uncle Sam's boys, Honey, and they are driving away the Japs."

She nodded her head gravely. "My," she said, "how many boys Uncle Sam has!"

By now American instructions were pouring in, informing the guerrillas of what was expected of them in preparation for the landings on Luzon.

The day before Christmas, the men left for a big guerrilla meeting. They expected to be back on the night of the twenty-eighth.

"If the ketchup bottle clinks, run and hide," Colonel Lloyd instructed me. "Do not shoot! If you can get away, go down to the river bank and follow it. Eventually you will run into the Negritoes, who will look after you."

Dian and I were left alone. For two days nothing happened, but on the twenty-sixth I heard the bottle go plunk. I have never seen such a look of fright on a child's face. It isn't a good thing to see.

She turned to me, her face quivering, but not making a sound.

"We've got to go, Honey," I whispered.

She nodded. "We mustn't forget baby," she said, so I picked up the doll Colonel Lloyd had made for her and for no particular reason took along the canteen and mess kit. I don't know why I did that because we didn't have a single thing to eat in the camp at the time. We lay flat behind a log and waited.

After a while I looked up cautiously. A kinky head was moving behind the bushes and a Negrito called out. He had a letter for Colonel Lloyd.

It was wonderful news! The next day Pedro was coming up and he was going to bring us two chickens. Two chickens! We would be able to have a real Christmas dinner when the men returned.

The next day the ketchup bottle clinked again, and Dian and I hid until I was sure it was Pedro Pamintuan. He not only brought us two chickens, but fresh vegetables, greens, and some bananas as well. That was such a feast as I had not seen in more months than I could count.

I hung the bananas from the roof, spread out the vegetables and greens, and tied the two chickens together under my bed. Colonel Reynolds might not be altogether happy about it when he came back, but no one could afford to be fussy when he had the prospect before him of a full meal.

The men were expected back on the twenty-eighth and I set about preparations for our feast. In the midst of them, I heard Dian yelling with excitement and looked up to see my chickens taking flight. I chased them like crazy but they kept getting out of reach and I began to cry. To think of food for two whole days and then see your dinner just get up and walk off was too much to bear.

There was no doubt that the chickens were more agile than I was, so I decided to play a waiting game. It worked pretty well. After a while, one of my strays gave up and came wandering back of its own accord. But the other had more of the spirit of adventure in it. I was after it again when the men came plodding wearily up the hill.

"Hey," I shouted, pointing to the chicken, "there goes our Christmas dinner!"

They threw off their fatigue and took out after the chicken, but with as little success as I had had. Then Reynolds reached for a gun and fired. He looked in awe at the result. "My God," he exclaimed, "oh, my God, how did I do that?"

The chicken had exploded. There was chicken everywhere we looked.

"Hey," roared Colonel Lloyd, "you took the wrong gun."

I was no Annie Oakley, and they had left a gun for me loaded with a dumdum bullet. "Even if you don't aim very well," they explained, "you are bound to do some damage with this — if you have to shoot."

We got to work and collected that chicken and put it in the pot, feathers and all, and boiled it. We could not waste food. We just figured that the fellow who got the most feathers would get the most chicken, and let it go at that.

Right after the New Year, we started moving slowly down the hill. But we had to move our first camp because when Colonel Lloyd followed us he discovered marks on the trees made by the Japanese in 1941. We had pitched camp only a few feet from their trail, so he made us move on again.

The men were gone most of the time now, rounding up the Filipino scouts and heading for Lingayen beach to drive the Japanese away and protect the American landings. And if they had done nothing else, the guerrillas would have justified their existence then, because they saved many American lives. Our forces were almost a mile inland before they encountered a single Jap.

Lloyd wanted me to stay behind. "You have done enough," he said. "Suppose you get killed — I could not take care of Dian."

But I had to go.

"You have a memory like a victrola record," he said. "I think the things you know about the collaboration and spies should be put on record." So he relieved me of medical duty and gave me a special assignment — making a list of names of collaborators for Counter Intelligence. Within a short time I has between twenty-five and thirty pages, in which I put down what Colonel Duckworth and Colonel Mack had written from the prison camps, listed the executions I had witnessed, and drew up lists of collaborators and spies, as well as of those who had backed us.

Naturally, I did not stop my medical duty just because of another assignment. If someone needed help I gave it, and this included being midwife half a dozen times during that slow progress of ours down the hill. When the wounded could travel, they came to me; otherwise, I went to them.

And one day Colonel Lloyd came to me with a letter addressed to the head of the United States Army Forces in the Pacific. "Mrs. Utinsky," it said, "perhaps has wider and more intimate knowledge than any other person of conditions which existed in the prison camps on Luzon, and it is believed that the first-hand information she possesses of brutal, inhuman treatment of prisoners might effectively be used in America to stimulate the war effort."

"The time has come," Colonel Lloyd explained, "when you must be taken care of by the American forces. Show this to the first American soldier you see and he will take you to the commanding officer, who will take you to General MacArthur."

At the time I paid little attention. I still could not believe the Americans were so near.

But on February 5, word came to start marching. The Yanks had made a four-point landing! I was instructed to go down to Tala, where I would meet Colonel Abad and the Second Regiment of guerrillas. From there Abad would arrange to have me taken to the American Army.

There never was a day like that. It seemed to me that I had wings, that nothing would ever tire me again. It was like a wild march of triumph.

Dian and I, the kitten and the doll, started down the mountain with a convoy of Negritoes. As we passed through each native barrio, the people would run out screaming, "Your people have come! God bless you, Miss U!"

Damacio, the elderly Negrito, asked by gestures how I wanted to travel to Tala. There was a choice of routes. One, his gestures indicated, was long but comparatively easy to travel. The second, described by two brief up and down motions, was shorter but it was straight up and down hill. I voted for the shorter route and off we went. I got more than I bargained for.

After months of bamboo forests, I didn't ask for a road, but I did expect some sort of trail. But the Negritoes, under Damacio's energetic orders, took their bolos and began to hack a path right through the forest. When the first man had cut a place big enough to slide into, he went ahead and we wedged our way into the small space after him, traveling single file. It was bad enough where the way was level, but when we had to go straight down the side of a mountain, I thought it would be impossible.

The Negritoes, moving at an incredible rate of speed, and sure-footed, hacked and cut a path, hanging onto trees to keep from pitching down. When they had cleared a big enough space, I sailed down the mountain, sitting down, bumping over brush and hastily cut bamboo logs, hanging on to Damacio.

Once the pace was too much even for him. We were coasting down at a terrific rate when he slipped at the edge of a ravine and rolled with me to the bottom of it. We landed on a flat rock under about three feet of water. While I was fighting for breath, Damacio leaped to his feet, dancing with rage, yelling one of his few English phrases, "Goddam, Miss U!"

When we had to go up the mountain, it was worse. There didn't seem to be a slope at all, just a straight mountain face. But the Negrito in the lead pulled himself up, hanging precariously to the limb of a tree. With his free hand he would take hold of one of my hands and the man below would take my feet. While one pulled and one pushed, I was dragged up, foot by foot, on my stomach.

That was a trail any self-respecting mountain goat would have turned his back on. Only a monkey could have done it. But we made it, and all the time my mind was singing, "The Yanks have come! The Yanks are here!" The prison camps would open and the starving men would come. There would be an end to torture and violent death and fear.

At four in the afternoon, we came down into Tala, where Colonel Abad and the Second Regiment were waiting.

Colonel Abad hailed me. "I heard you were coming. You had better have something to eat."

"That's what you think," I said. "I'll never insult my stomach with rice again. I'm going on."

I marched on with the Second Regiment to Orani. That day I could walk faster than I ever did in all my life. When we got to Orani, there were signs of battle everywhere. The Americans had been through earlier in the day.

"Let's go on," I implored Colonel Abad. It seemed to me that I could not wait to be with the Americans.

"Not tonight," he said. "It is dark; the bridges are gone; the country is full of retreating Japanese."

I did not much like the idea of meeting the Japanese in the dark so I decided reluctantly to spend the night in Orani. The Negritoes climbed up in the tower of the church and rang the bells loudly and joyously; then they waved goodbye to me and started back into the hills.

We put up for the night in the municipal building. It was too dark to see, which was just as well, as I needed sleep. Dian and I curled up in a corner.

At the crack of dawn I woke up and looked around me. It was a place of horror, a bloody mess. There were hair and blood and brains all over the floor. Apparently, the Japanese had used it for a prison. How many people had been massacred there it was impossible to guess from the ghastly evidence. They had butchered their prisoners as our troops were coming in. Even under the seats there was clotted blood.

I was sickened and I got Dian out of there in a hurry. "Let's go," I said to Colonel Abad.

He shook his head. "Not yet," he said. "It isn't safe. There are Japanese snipers all the way between here and the American troops. There isn't a chance to get through."

"But I've got to go."

"You've stayed alive this long," he pointed out. "Why take a chance on being picked off now by a sniper? That doesn't make sense. Wait until the way is safe."

"I'm going."

Colonel Abad shrugged his shoulders. "Lieutenant," he said, "you are on your own," and he washed his hands of me.

I bargained for a horse that had two speeds, slow and stop, a skinny nag with a home-made saddle and no belly band. I couldn't put my feet in the stirrups because the men's shoes I was wearing were so enormous. I was wearing a dress made out of a red curtain from a native woman's hut, a big wide native hat, a gun belt Major Reynolds had made for my .38, and socks knitted out of string. All in all, I was quite a sight.

The Filipino who owned the horse agreed to go with me and carry Dian until we found the Americans. I guaranteed that when we got there the Americans would give him ten dollars in United States currency. I was being pretty free with Uncle Sam's money, but I was in a lavish mood. The Filipino said he didn't care about the money if the Americans would only give him supper and breakfast.

I climbed on the horse and we started off. When we came to the rivers, Pedro would take hold of the horse — there was no bridle, just a rope around his neck — and lead him. I would hang on to his mane for dear life to keep from pitching over his head. When we came out of the river I hung on like mad to keep from sliding off his tail.

And all the time we watched the roads and the trees and the bushes, alert for Japanese snipers.

We had been traveling for hours when I saw soldiers ahead, crouching in a ditch by the side of the road. They were wearing green uniforms! I stopped the horse, feeling cold and sick all over. Green meant Japs! I had to think fast, to concoct a story that would sound convincing. It had to be the very best story of my life, or it would be my last one.

Then one of the uniforms stood up and inside it was a long weedy boy with a flaming red head.

"Oh, Honey," I sobbed to Dian, "only a Yank grows like that!"

I loped down the road. The redhead looked at me and yelled, "Hey, Les, there's a white woman!"

"It's a mirage," grunted another Yank, not bothering to look up.

"Bet she's from Texas," called the redhead. "Look at her pack a gun and ride that horse!"

They were all on their feet now, staring at me. And all at once they began to sing a song I had never heard before: "Pistol-packing mama, lay that pistol down!"

"Uncle Sam's boys?" asked Dian.

"Uncle Sam's boys," I told her. "Hey boys, I'm coming down."

I came off the horse, saddle and all, and fell into the arms of the Sixth Army.

This Flower—Safety

I don't remember much about those first few excited minutes while the Sixth Army and I exchanged rapid questions and answers as fast as we could talk. I was sitting on the ground, working on one of those monstrous shoes of mine, when a soldier came up.

"Hi, Buddy," I said carelessly, "have you got a pair of pliers?"

He shut his eyes, hoping, obviously, that when he opened them again I wouldn't be there.

He opened them again. "Aren't you an American woman?"

"Yes," I said. "I want some pliers."

He stood blinking at me. "Why?"

"There's a nail in my shoe."

He bent over to help me and I was the one who blinked. I saw for the first time that he was a colonel.

"What are you doing out here?" he asked. "It's no place for a woman. There's a war on."

I pulled out Lloyd's letter and handed it to him, and went on wrestling with that nail.

He read it slowly. "Woman guerrilla!" he exclaimed. "Goddam, what is this war coming to?" He thought for a moment. "You can't stay here," he said. "I'll telephone for transportation. We'll send you on to Dinalupihan."

"I don't need transportation," I declared, and I started on, accompanied by a few soldiers, my Filipino with the horse, Dian, the yellow kitten, and the doll — and my .38.

We had not gone far when some men came racing toward us with a stretcher. Colonel Houseman had telephoned for transportation. That was it I firmly refused to climb on that stretcher and be carried, so I went on walking. All along the line, the sight of a white woman practically brought operations to a halt, and more men kept joining the procession.

After a while, a carretela came along. It was an improvement on the stretcher, anyhow, and as long as they were insistent on my riding, I climbed in and the men walked alongside. By the time I reached Dinalupihan, I had collected so many soldiers that I practically had an army with me.

And all of them were showering me with questions. What was I doing here? What was it like being a guerrilla? I answered them patiently for a while, then I said firmly, "Look here, I've answered enough questions. How about you answering a few? First I want to know how long skirts are now?"

Pictures came out of their pockets like a shower of falling autumn leaves, and I looked at their girls. "They're wearing them shorter," I said.

"Shortage of material," one of them explained. He added thoughtfully, "Or so they say."

When I came into Dinalupihan with my private army, the troops and I looked at each other with mutual amazement.

"Jeepers," someone yelled, "there's a white woman!"

I stood with my mouth open. I couldn't take it in. Four years before, I had seen the American flag lowered; I had watched American prisoners shambling through the streets of Manila on their way to prison; I had seen airstrips from which a plane never rose. Now I was seeing the unbelievable thing that had happened to the American Army in that short space of time. There were tanks and guns I had never seen before, equipment I had never dreamed of, planes that did not look real. Overhead a big plane was dropping supplies and I stood watching, with the stuff falling all around me, until a man grabbed me by the arm and ran for cover.

"Hey," he protested, "you'll get yourself killed! One of those boxes will land right on your head."

But I had to watch. You can dream and imagine what victory will be like — and I had done that for months and months — but never had I conceived of anything like the sight before me. I had spent years of my life in Army circles but it seemed impossible that it could have been so transformed, that it could have created these miracles.

Someone took me to Colonel Skelton, who was in charge of operations at Dinalupihan. "Lieutenant Utinsky," he said, "you look as though you need food." (For weeks everyone tried to feed me.) "But at least you will have time for coffee. There will be a plane here for you in a few minutes."

Soon I would wake up. None of this could be true.

"There must be some mistake," I told him. "No one even knows I am here."

Colonel Skelton explained. "This morning Colonel Lloyd and Colonel Boone were through here. They told me about you. They said you were supposed to come along with Colonel Abad and the Second Regiment.

They thought Colonel Abad might hold off until we'd cleared out the snipers, but they said you would be here if you had to steal a horse." He looked out and grinned. "I see you have the horse."

I laughed and explained that I had acquired Pedro and his nag by a lavish promise of breakfast and supper at the expense of the United States Army, and ten dollars as well. The Army kept my promise for me.

"Major," Colonel Skelton said, "will you escort Lieutenant Utinsky to her plane?"

I marched out with great dignity, wearing my big straw hat, flapping man's shoes, and my red curtain dress. But before we reached the road, a newspaperman came rushing at me and all my dignity vanished. I was terrified. It had been a long time since anyone had rushed at me in a friendly way and I guess my nerves were none too good. He apologized, but the major firmly refused to let him come near or to ask me any questions.

There was a tiny airplane that looked like a bug, circling around. It came down and settled right in the middle of the road. The pilot jumped out and turned it around by the tail. Then he strolled over and looked at me and Dian. His eyebrows shot up. He swallowed hard. "I'm supposed to pick up an American nurse," he said. "I guess you're it."

"I'm it."

He balked at taking the kitten and we parted with it there. Even Dian was reconciled, for she was as drunk with excitement as I was. I had never been in a plane in my life, and the pilot talked to me, pointing out points of interest as we went on toward MacArthur's headquarters.

Once he dropped down so I could see a brown ribbon winding over the mountain.

"That's where the real fighting is going on," he said. "Want to go closer and look at it?"

"No," I told him sharply, "I've seen all the fighting I want in my life."

"I'll fly you over the gulf," he said, "and let you see the ships."

And he did. I looked down at the fleet riding at anchor and my eyes stung with tears. I was so proud I could not bear it. The Yanks had come back — and how!

As we circled over the camp, the pilot said, "Watch the expression on the men's faces when a woman steps out of this plane. It ought to be good."

I got out and it was like a slow moving picture. The soldiers simply came to a dead halt. They stopped with food halfway to their mouths, as though they had been frozen. No one said a word. The pilot, like everyone else who saw me, thought I was on the brink of starvation, and he took me to a man who was slicing sandwiches. The knife stopped right in the middle of the loaf and the man's jaw dropped.

When I reached headquarters, Lieutenant General Charles P. Hall sent for food at once. He read Colonel Lloyd's letter and asked for my black and white lists, which I turned over to him. In return, he let me see a list of men who had been liberated from Cabanatuan. They were in an evacuation camp nearby. The Rangers had freed 511 of them. Every day, twenty officers and eighty enlisted men were being flown to Leyte and sent on from there by ship to the United States.

I wanted to see my men before they left the Philippines and the general put in a telephone call to Colonel Graham, the medical officer in charge of evacuation.

"There is a Miss U here," he began, "who would like…"

There was a rattle of speech at the other end and he turned around to repeat the conversation. "Colonel Graham says to send you there at once — before Colonel Duckworth gets apoplexy!"

But first I was to have a night's sleep — in a bed with sheets and an air mattress! I jumped up and down on it and nearly bounced right out the window. I had a bath and more food and clothing. I was clean.

And I saw myself in a mirror. For a long time, I stood there, getting acquainted with Guerrilla Officer Utinsky. I couldn't find Peggy Doolin at all. No one, looking at my passport, would have believed I was the same woman.

Weight — 120 pounds (Now I weighed 85.)

Height — 5 feet (I had shrunk an inch from torture.)

Hair — brown. (Mine was gray.)

Identifying marks — none. (My legs were covered with blue scars from the gangrene that had set in from the bamboo bench. I had a broken jaw which had never been set. I could not lift my arms very far because of all those days when I had been hung. There was a curious lump under my left breast which was caused by the breastbone splitting from torture.)

That was the first night I had gone to bed in safety in years. No Japanese could get me here. Nothing would bother me until morning. Uncle Sam's boys were on guard. I slept.

The next morning, Major Ike Kampmann, of San Antonio, was waiting for me, and after breakfast we climbed aboard a huge plane and flew to

Santa Rosa. From there we drove by jeep to the Calacio evacuation camp, where the Cabanatuan boys were resting.

When I reached the evacuation camp, they were waiting for me. For the first time, I met Colonel Duckworth, with whom I had worked so long, to whom I had written so many letters. He was a handsome man and his right arm was in a sling.

"Miss U," he said, "this is a day I have looked forward to for a long time."

"What happened to your arm, Colonel?"

He grinned. "You know," he said, "when the Japs took us prisoner, I fell in a ditch and broke my left arm. When the Yanks came to let us out, I was so excited I fell in another ditch and broke my right arm in three places."

He told me then what had happened. Seventeen days before the Americans came to liberate the prisoners, the Japanese officers announced, "You are no longer prisoners — if you stay inside the barbed wire, you won't be bothered. If you go out, you will be shot."

The men were dying of starvation and that was the last act of the Japanese, trying to kill them oft before the Americans came.

The Japanese left and Duckworth and his men rushed to the Japanese quarters. They found tins of canned food, milk, fish — much of the stuff stolen from American Red Cross packages. The Japanese had left in such haste that there were still pigs roasting in the oven.

"We all lost our heads," Colonel Duckworth admitted. "As a doctor I should have known better. We snatched at food and wolfed it down, growling and groaning over it. There wasn't a man of us who didn't get sick."

After that first mad stuffing on food, however, the men were warned to eat only a little at a time. Otherwise, after their long period of semi-starvation, they would kill themselves. Incredible as it may seem, every one of those men put on from twenty-five to forty pounds in the seventeen days before the Rangers came. Even so, they looked like walking skeletons when they were released.

As my men — I can't help thinking of them as that — were being shipped out so rapidly, I was moved by plane and jeep from one evacuation camp to another so that I could meet as many of them as possible and check up on what had happened to them.

At the next camp I met Colonel Oliver. He too told me the story of the seventeen days between the withdrawal of the Japanese and the arrival of the Yanks.

They could hear the fighting going on, the sound of the artillery. They saw the planes which circled over the prison, coming so low the pilots waved at the men behind the barbed wire.

One dark night they heard people coming and saw tracer bullets over the wall. They all fell in a ditch which served as a latrine.

A man came up to the gate with a rifle. "You men come out of there," he called. "We have come to liberate you."

The Japanese who guarded the Americans frequently spoke flawless English and Colonel Oliver said, "It's a trap."

A private lifted his head out of the foul-smelling ditch and called, "Where you all from?"

The man outside the fence promptly named an obscure little southwestern town.

The private scrambled to his feet. "That's good enough for me, men," he decided. "I'm going with him."

It was the Rangers.

While I was talking to Colonel Oliver, a Colonel Hill came up and shook hands with me.

"I knew your husband well," he told me. "We served in the First World War together. I was with him in Siberia. We resigned from the Army together; we were at Bataan together, and later captured together in the tunnel on Corregidor." He hesitated for a moment. "I was with him in Cabanatuan when he died."

And Colonel Oliver wrote a gracious letter in which he said:

"It is the opinion of the undersigned that Brevet Lieutenant Utinsky did more than any other one person for the morale and physical well being of the Allied Prisoners of War held at Camp O'Donnell and Prison Camp No. I., Cabanatuan. (Signed) Alfred Oliver, Colonel Chaplain Corps, U. S. Army."

I saw many men who had been only names to me for years; I heard of others whom I had missed because they had already been flown out to Leyte. I learned of those who had died.

But the most tragic thing of all was hearing of the men who had been sunk by American planes while they were being shipped as prisoners of war to Japan. That they should have been kept alive until almost the very end, and that then they should have died, through some appalling error, at the hands of their own countrymen, seemed unbearable.

MacArthur's headquarters sent me to the Red Cross at Gerona, where they assigned me a tent and offered to keep me busy, though I had never seen eye to eye with the Red Cross and preferred to work in my own way. I got more done. But General Courtney Whitney told me to stay there. He thought, I suppose, that otherwise I would get into trouble.

I didn't want to stay there. I was wild to get to Manila.

Everyone said no. Manila had not been taken yet; the fighting was centered there. But the Counter Intelligence Corps got in touch with me and asked if I would work with them. Would I? I gave them my records on collaborators and worked with them by day, eating with the medical officers.

As they kept moving up, I found a way to move along with them — sometimes even ahead of them. I went by jeep to San Miguel and then thumbed a ride on a duck to Tarlac, where, in a hospital tent, I ran into Colonel Lloyd again. Then on to San Fernando, where I ran into the C.I.C. gang again.

We were near Manila now and I wanted to go to Cabanatuan and find my husband's grave. Lieutenant James McElhinney told me that he knew where it was and he escorted Dian and me to the prison. It was empty now. There was no one left but the dead.

We came at length to a big mound. "Here," he said. I didn't understand. "But why," I asked, "is it so large?"

"Your husband isn't alone," he explained. "There are fourteen people in that hole."

In a way that was as bitter a shock as I had had since the moment when I knew Jack was dead. Since then, I have tried the best I knew how to explain to people here that it is pointless to attempt to bring back home the bodies of the dead. No one now can possibly know what bodies are being moved. No identification can be made. Let those men, who were so terribly tired, rest at last where they are. It is better that way.

No one would let me enter Manila, but I piled on a truck, one of a convoy of fifty that was headed that way. Just outside, the convoy was halted.

"I want to go in," I told the M.P. who had stopped us.

"You can't go in there," he said. "Manila has not been taken yet. It is dangerous."

"Well, what do you think I have been doing for the past four years?" I snapped. "Looking for danger?"

"Lady," he said wearily, "thirty-five thousand people want to come in."

"I'm the one who is coming in," I said firmly.

He took another look at me and then yelled for help. An officer came up and after a little discussion admitted me. I looked around me. Manila! I was back again. An M.P. came up and stared at me.

"Lady," he demanded, "have you a permit to carry that gun?"

End of an Adventure

That night I slept once more in Manila and early the following morning General Whitney's son found me.

"Everyone has been looking for you," he said. "Now you stay right here. Don't move until I come back."

So I sat under a tree and waited. In a short time General Whitney came up, and shook his head. "You travel faster than the Army," he declared.

Eugene Smith was assigned as my aide and I got the necessary papers to move around Manila, a permit to carry the gun I had used for almost a year, and I was assigned to the Counter Intelligence, helping to run down collaborators and

And best of all — that afternoon a cable arrived from my son, the first word I had had from him in all the long months since Pearl Harbor, asking for news of my whereabouts.

My first job was to find Dian's mother, who was now interned in Santo Tomas, and return her baby to her. This proved to be harder for all of us than I had anticipated. You cannot take care of a child for so long a time without coming to love it, and I hated to let Dian go. So far as she was concerned, she no longer knew her mother, and she cried at having to leave me. It was hard on her mother too, when she discovered that her own child no longer recognized her or felt at ease with her. Today, Dian and her parents are living in safety at last on the Pacific Coast and all is well with them.

Armed with the necessary permits, I went out to inspect Manila, while a handful of G.I.'s came stringing along. At first I could not believe it. Manila was in ruins. Where buildings had stood, there were gaping holes. There were dead bodies all over the place.

"Don't come across," an M.P. said when the soldiers and I reached the center of old Manila.

"Why not?"

"There is fighting still going on."

"Never mind," I told him. "I've come a long way to see our boys drive the Japanese back." I showed him my papers that proved I was looking for information and evidence about collaborators, and he let us through.

At that time I was so filled with bitter hatred for the Japanese, after having seen with my own eyes the hideous things they had done to soldiers and non-combatants alike, that I felt there was no punishment harsh enough for them. There was no Japanese, man, woman or child, for whom I felt the slightest sympathy. It was not until I saw pictures of the Yanks stopping in the midst of the fighting, to pick up a little Japanese baby and dry its tears, that I began to get back a little perspective. Not that I'll ever forget. I won't.

Manila was a charnelhouse, with bodies everywhere. We even found the corpses of women and children lying in the swamps. War has a kind of drunken exhilaration about it, but the aftermath of war is horrible beyond words.

Here and there, as we walked through buildings inspecting the damage, we saw places on the walls where ropes had hung with slip knots and pulleys.

"What are these for?" one of the soldiers asked me.

"Those are the gadgets they hang you by," I explained. And I demonstrated how the wrists were tied to the ropes; how the pulley jerked you up and dropped you down again.

"How do you know?" he asked curiously.

"Because they hung me in gadgets like this for the best part of a month," I said.

I began to get a picture of what had happened in Manila during those last days before the Americans arrived. The Japanese had slaughtered their prisoners wholesale — and it must have been doubly bitter to die with the rescuers so near — gathering up the sick and the maimed, those who had been comparatively free to come and go within the limits of Manila up to that time. It seemed as though the Japanese could not rest until every available American was dead. I have in my possession pictures of the cell in which I was imprisoned in Fort Santiago. It is stacked with dead bodies.

With some men from the signal corps I went to Camp Nichols, thinking I could explain better on the spot what had been done there. Everything had been burned. A native woman came up during our inspection. "I remember you," she said. "You used to hide in the hut over there to watch what was going on in the camp."

All that watching I had done then, agonizing as it had been, served its purpose now, for I had information that no one else could have obtained.

The Filipina woman pointed out some of the graves of the prisoners. We counted twenty-seven of them in the field and found a lot more behind the school. Most of these deaths went down on the record as caused by malaria. In many cases, the Japanese tried to force American medical officers to sign documents, saying our men had died of malaria.

Then we went on to the Malate Convent, which had been a refuge and a place of peace during those early days in Manila. Nothing was standing but the walls of the church. There were parts of bodies all over the place, and blood was spattered everywhere. Everyone was dead.

"When did this happen?" I asked.

"Just as we were coming in," one of the men answered bitterly.

So they were gone, all of the priests who had worked so gallantly for us. All of them, of course, had known the risks they ran; they had known, at the time I made my escape from Manila, that their names, like mine, were on the Japanese death lists. But they had chosen to remain until they were killed — shot, burned, crucified — and they had stayed gladly. They were, in their quiet way, the most magnificent men I ever knew.

While we were walking through the ruins of the school, I noticed that part of a wall was still standing and there flashed into my mind a picture, long forgotten, of a talk I had had with Father Lalor early in my efforts to raise money for the prisoners.

At that time, I had sold all my personal belongings, with the exception of a wrist watch which I did not wear because the Japanese were wild about wrist watches and took them away from us. But I could not bear to sell it because it was the last present Jack had given me, but one time when I was in pressing need of a certain sum of money — I forget now what was needed: food, drugs, clothing — and the watch did not bring in as much as I had to have, as usual I had gone to the convent to discuss my difficulties with Father Lalor.

He shook his head. He did not have the money and at the moment he did not know of anyone from whom he could get it.

All of a sudden he got up and left me. When he returned, he handed me a beautiful watch, which had been presented to him. "If you can part with your watch, I can part with mine," he said.

I refused but he would not accept my refusal, and he pressed it upon me. Reluctantly I took it along. When I got back to my apartment that day, one of my assistants, Phyliss Dunn, came in and saw the watch. I explained what had happened.

"You can't sell Father Lalor's watch," she declared, and she offered to lend me money with the watch as security, about half of what I needed. She did not take the watch with her.

A little later, Mr. de Guzman, owner of the Congress Hotel, came in and offered to make up the rest of the sum on the same watch. When he left, it was still on my table. So I took it back to Father Lalor and told him that he had, after all, contributed the amount of money I needed. Later, Don Luis Teehankee redeemed my watch for me and I gave it to Father Lalor to hide for me, so that I would not lose it.

It was that day that Father Lalor said, "Come with me. I want to show you something." He showed me a secret hiding place in the wall and taught me to open it.

"One of these days," he said, "Something may happen to me — to all of us here. When that time comes, someone should know about this hiding place. We keep in it the few valuables we have."

While we stood looking at the wall, I told the G.I.'s the story of Father Lalor's watch and the secret hiding place. Then, recalling his instructions, I opened it. There was nothing inside. Yes, my groping fingers discovered, there was something. I reached farther and pulled out two watches — Father Lalor's and mine.

By this time, I had become a thorn in the flesh of the Counter Intelligence, because I kept hammering away at the American newspaper woman. It was becoming an obsession with me. For four years I had known that this American newspaper woman was a spy. I had told the guerrillas about her long before I ever joined them in the hills, but they refused to do anything about her because they said any action they took would only throw suspicion on me.

No evidence, the Army said over and over. Yet this woman was responsible for betraying to the Japanese many of the Miss U organization as well as other Americans. Their murder rested squarely on her shoulders.

She turned in to the enemy A. F. Duggleby, vice president of the Benguet Gold Mine; Mr. Carroll C. Grinnell, of General Electric; Clifford Larsen — this latter, as it proved, was a mistake based on similarity of names. The Japanese were looking for a Chris Larsen, who was a Standard Oil man and known to be on terms with Ernest Johnson. And she had turned in Ernest Johnson, Maritime Commission officer, the Brave Heart of our organization. The Japanese had put them all to death.

Ernest Johnson had remained in the hospital until the Americans drew closer to the Philippines and the Japanese spread wide their nets and gathered in all the Americans. He was taken to Santo Tomas and the American newspaper woman went in also, presumably as a prisoner. She became very friendly with Johnson, who thought there was no reason to suspect an American who was a fellow prisoner. So he talked to her and she learned that he was connected with the guerrillas and that he had been aiding American prisoners of war.

Another of the names I had turned over to the Counter Intelligence Corps was that of a Filipina woman spy, and I was sent out to bring her in. On the way I stopped at a hospital where some of the ex-prisoners were patients, knowing that one of them had pictures of the woman taken with Japanese soldiers. I talked to the patients for some time, getting evidence on executions, the names of the Japanese officers involved, and so forth.

Then, taking a soldier with me because I was afraid to go to the house alone, I went to pick up the woman. At that time, everything was still in such confusion that arrests were informal affairs. I came out of the house with my prisoner and as I had no means of transportation, I thumbed a ride back. By chance, the car that stopped was filled with my old guerrilla friends.

When I got back to headquarters, no one seemed to be around, so I sat down on a box under a tree waiting for some officer to come along and take my prisoner off my hands.

While I was waiting, a young Lieutenant came up to me.

"Lieutenant Utinsky?"

"Major Labatt is looking for you. They have been broadcasting for you and here you sit, right in front of the place."

I went inside and while I was waiting for Major Labatt, a woman came in to get the passes which were necessary in order to move about Manila. She sat down and I realized that she was watching me. At last she jumped to her feet and came over to me eagerly.

"Miss U," she gushed, "I have heard of the wonderful work you have done. I'm so glad you came through alive. I am the American newspaper woman."

"I'm damned if you're not!" I said, and I went straight to the C.I.C. officer. "I want that woman arrested. She is a spy."

And there I ran up against the problem of "no evidence — no arrest" again. What infuriated me was the fact that while the woman went about freely, the Counter Intelligence was keeping suspicious eyes on Max Kummer. He was a German, wasn't he? The only personal request I made at any time was that Max Kummer should not be interned. German or not German, everything I had done for the prisoners of war I owed to Max Kummer and his wife. At great personal risk, they had made possible every single step of the way.

Arrangements were being made for me to return to the States but I refused to go. "I will not leave the Philippines," I declared, "until that woman is arrested."

And one day I was told that another complaint had come in about my suspect. Ernest Johnson's son, Thor Johnson, arrived in Manila with the American forces the day a grave was dug up. In it Ernest Johnson's body was found with fourteen others. Johnson was wearing a blindfold and he had been shot in the back. Another man had his throat cut. There was a Filipino Army officer, an unknown charity nun and Grinnell, Duggleby and Larsen, all with hands tied behind them, and still wearing blindfolds. The bodies lying underneath could no longer be identified.

Johnson's son Thor got busy and at last my suspect was arrested. A woman was assigned to search her.

"I know she wears a belt with papers in it," I said, and they took her off to strip her and go over her clothes.

Time passed while I paced up and down. At length a report came back. "The woman does not wear a belt. There are no papers."

I was sunk; but there simply had to be papers. "Try again," I said. "Search the hems of her clothes; rip out every seam."

The officer who brought the next report was grinning. "We found the papers," he said. "She wore a double brassiere, and the papers were sewed between the two pieces of cloth."

"What was in them?"

The grin grew broader. "The complete Japanese code."

Two days later I received a message from Major Hans Menzie, who was investigating the spy case. "You can return to the States, Miss U. She has confessed."

However, there was one more thing that had to be done before I could leave the Philippines. I had to find Lee. He sent word to me through a Filipina woman as to his whereabouts, and I went to see him. Before I went, I raised twenty dollars — all I could get my hands on — so he would have something to tide him over for a while.

When I found him, Lee, for once, did not scold. He beamed. He fumbled in his pockets and pulled out twenty dollars. "I raised it for you," he said. "I thought you would need it."

"You keep it," I told him. "I'll be all right."

"Have you got any money?" he demanded suspiciously.

"No," I admitted, "but I'll be all right. I am going home and something will happen."

Lee nodded his head. "Yes, Miss Peggy," he said. "For you something always happens."

Made in the USA
San Bernardino, CA
05 January 2018